curriculum
connections

Civil War

Home Front and the Economy

BROWN
BEAR
BOOKS

Published by Brown Bear Books Ltd

4877 N. Circulo Bujia
Tucson
AZ 85718
USA

First Floor
9–17 St. Albans Place
London N1 0NX
UK

© 2011 Brown Bear Books Ltd

ISBN: 978-1-936333-45-5

Managing Editor: Tim Cooke
Designer: Joan Curtis
Picture Researcher: Sophie Mortimer
Art Director: Jeni Child
Editorial Director: Lindsey Lowe

Library of Congress Cataloging-in-Publication Data

Home front and the economy / edited by Tim Cooke.
    p. cm. -- (Curriculum connections : Civil War)
Includes index.
Summary: "In an alphabetical almanac format, describes the civilian life during the U.S. Civil War"- Provided by publisher.
    ISBN 978-1-936333-45-5 (library binding)
1. United States--History--Civil War, 1861-1865-- Economic aspects. 2. United States--Economic conditions--To 1865. 3. United States--Social conditions--To 1865. I. Cooke, Tim, 1961- II. Title. III. Series.

HC105.6.H66 2012
973.7'1--dc22
                         2011005399

Picture Credits

Cover Image
Library of Congress

Library of Congress: 11,14, 18, 23, 29, 31, 34, 36, 44, 53, 58, 64, 70, 83, 88, 91, 93, 98, 102, 105; National Archives: 7, 40, 49, 62, 68, 77, 95; Robert Hunt Library: 16; Shutterstock: 74

Artwork © Brown Bear Books Ltd

Printed in the United States of America

Contents

Introduction

Civil War **forms part of the Curriculum Connections series. Each of the six volumes of the set covers a particular aspect of the conflict: Home Front and the Economy; Behind the Fighting; Weapons, Tactics, and Strategy; Politics; Battles and Campaigns; and People.**

About this set

Each volume in *Civil War* features illustrated chapters, providing in-depth information about each subject. The chapters are all listed in the contents pages of each book. Each volume can be studied to provide a comprehensive understanding of all aspects of the conflict. However, each chapter may also be studied independently.

Within each chapter there are two key aids to learning that are to be found in color sidebars located in the margins of each page:

Curriculum Context sidebars indicate to the reader that a subject has a particular relevance to certain key state and national history guidelines and curricula. They highlight essential information or suggest useful ways for students to consider a subject or to include it in their studies.

Glossary sidebars define key words within the text.

At the end of the book, a summary **Glossary** lists the key terms defined in the volume. There is also a list of further print and Web-based resources and a full volume index.

Fully captioned illustrations play an important role throughout the set, including photographs and explanatory maps.

About this book

Home Front and the Economy places the conflict that followed the secession of the Southern states in 1861 and the creation of the Confederacy in the context of its impact on daily life in the North and the South.

For many families in the North, far from the fighting, life went on much as normal. In the South, on the other hand, the war caused shortages of food and other goods. Many women were forced into work to replace men who were away fighting, while many children found their education interrupted by a lack of teachers.

One of the main causes of the war was economic: the reliance of the South on cotton and the reliance of the cotton plantations in turn on the "peculiar institution" of slavery. Despite Southern hopes, an embargo of cotton exports failed to force European nations to recognize the Confederacy. Instead, a Northern blockade of Southern ports stifled imports and exports and led to severe hardship.

When the conflict started, the North had the advantage in terms of resources and industry. Once the fighting began, the North's ability to produce more gunpowder weapons and ammunition, medicines, and supplies greatly benefited its military strategy. Its far greater network of railroad tracks, meanwhile, allowed it to move large numbers of troops rapidly over long distances. In one of the earliest examples of industrialized warfare, the North's economic superiority would prove decisive.

Agriculture

In the North farmers were able to profit from the high demand for food created by the war. In the South, however, battles devastated farmland, and the freeing of the slaves ended a prosperous way of life for Southern farmers and planters.

Curriculum Context

The differences between agrarian development in the North and the South are studied in some curricula.

Curriculum Context

Some curricula ask students to understand the significance of cotton in the Southern economy before the war.

Conscription

The compulsory drafting of individuals for military service.

When the Civil War started on April 12, 1861, more than half the United States population lived on farms. Agriculture made up three-quarters of exports. In the South large-scale farmers—planters—used slaves to produce cotton, sugarcane, and tobacco, while small-scale farmers grew cotton for market and corn for their family. In the North farmers raised wheat and corn to feed horses, cattle, and hogs. Dairy farmers provided milk for city dwellers.

Feeding the armies

The Civil War created a great demand for food to feed both armies. In the South, Confederate leaders urged farmers to raise more corn, wheat, and livestock and less cotton. Cotton could not be sold because the Union blockade of Southern ports limited shipments. The blockade also limited the South's imports of food. Many Southern farmers did plant more corn to feed people and livestock.

The Confederate government needed farmers and men to serve in the army. The Confederacy passed the first of three conscription acts on April 16, 1862. Southern men aged between 18 and 50 had to leave their farms. Only planters who held public office or who owned at least 20 slaves were exempt. As men left, agricultural production declined. Production suffered as slaves became reluctant to work as they anticipated their freedom, particularly after the Emancipation Proclamation on January 1, 1863, granted freedom to slaves in all states in rebellion.

Food shortages in the South

By 1863, the South experienced food shortages. In April, high food prices and shortages caused a bread riot in Richmond, Virginia, when a mob of women shouting "Bread or Blood" plundered stores for food. Soon other Confederate cities experienced food riots, and shortages spread to the army.

With demand high, Southern farmers tried to profit from the war by asking high prices. They were undercut by demand from the government. Farmers complained that officials forced them to sell produce too cheaply or took produce without paying. Some officials offered a piece of paper that only promised payment by the Confederate government. As a result, some Southern farmers hid their crops and livestock; others refused to accept Confederate money. When Union troops arrived in the South, they also took produce. They destroyed farm implements and railroads, making it more difficult to produce and distribute food in the South.

Slaves sort through cotton in South Carolina in 1861. Southern cotton production fell during the war as farmers concentrated on growing food for the army instead.

The Great Beefsteak Raid

Texas cattlemen supplied beef to Southerners east of the Mississippi River until the summer of 1862, when the Union navy took control of the river. Short of cattle, the Confederates were reduced to cattle raids on Union troops. On September 16, 1864, General Wade Hampton and his cavalrymen appeared at Coggins Point in the rear of the Union army on the James River and carried off the entire beef supply of 2,486 cattle. The "Great Beefsteak Raid," as it was called, brought joy and relief to the hungry Rebels. One soldier wrote home, "We are now having Yankee beef every day."

Sisters of the soldiers

With so many men away, women and children often worked in the fields, tended livestock, and sold produce. In 1863 women harvested most of the wheat crop in South Carolina. One observer called them "brave and faithful women who are worthy to be sisters of the soldiers of our army." Even so, much of the heavy work could not be completed. Production decreased dangerously when the army and people most needed food. Confederate policy did not help. The government urged ironworks to make guns rather than the plows, reapers, and corn shellers that were needed to produce more food.

Curriculum Context

The differences between agriculture in the North and the South are often studied among the causes of the Civil War.

The war in the North

The experience in the North was different. Troops took all the crops in Virginia, but Northern farmlands were largely untouched. Although about 40 percent of Union army conscripts, aged between 18 and 35, were farmers or farmers' sons, agricultural production did not decline. Older farmers, immigrants, discharged veterans, and women took their places in the fields.

The North experienced only temporary and minor shortages of agricultural labor. Northern farmers used profits from high agricultural prices to buy labor-saving machinery which could be operated by farm women to save on the cost of hiring workers at harvest time.

Northern farmers easily met their food needs. Between 1861 and 1865 the North produced a food surplus, exporting an average of 27 million bushels of wheat annually, a dramatic increase from less than 8 million bushels from 1856 to 1860. Farmers produced more oats, potatoes, and butter. Ohio farmers increased wool production to meet the demand for blankets and uniforms and to cover the loss of Southern cotton.

The end of slavery

When the war ended in 1865, Southern farmers faced many problems. In areas such as Virginia, Georgia, Tennessee, Mississippi, Louisiana, and the coastal area of the Carolinas, farms lay in ruins, fields abandoned, livestock killed or captured, and farm equipment worn out or destroyed. They were not reimbursed for commodities taken by Confederate officials or the Union. When the war ended and all slaves were freed, Southern planters lost at least $1.5 billion from their investment in slave labor. Agricultural production almost ceased. In 1861 Southern farmers and planters produced 4.5 million bales of cotton, but only 299,000 bales in 1864. Finally, 260,000 Confederate soldiers, mostly farmers, had been killed. Overall, the Civil War brought prosperity to most Northern farmers while it caused hardship for Southern farmers and planters.

Reimburse
To pay someone financial compensation.

Curriculum Context
Many states expect students to understand the economic problems facing the South at the end of the war and the start of Reconstruction.

Agricultural Reform

The Union Congress passed three important agricultural acts in 1862 that would affect farming in the North and South after the war. Congress created the United States Department of Agriculture, which soon became the most important scientific agency devoted to improving agriculture. In the same year it also passed the Morrill Land-Grant College Act, which authorized the creation of at least one college in each state where agriculture and mechanical arts would be taught in order to improve farm life. Finally, Congress approved the Homestead Act, which provided 160 acres of public domain free to any head of a household, male or female, who would live on it for five years and make improvements. This expanded agricultural production into the vast western territories and new states and led to the opening up of new territories.

Blockades and Blockade-runners

In the war at sea Union warships tried to cut off the Confederacy's overseas trade by sealing off 3,000 miles (4,830 km) of Southern coastline. Challenging the Union blockade were fast, specially designed vessels called blockade-runners.

On April 19, 1861, President Lincoln proclaimed a naval blockade of the Deep South states of Texas, Louisiana, Florida, Georgia, and South Carolina. On April 27 he extended it to include North Carolina and Virginia.

Curriculum Context

Some curricula ask students to understand the influence on the conflict of geographical factors such as the extended coastline of the South.

At first the blockade existed only on paper. The Union navy did not have enough vessels to patrol the 187 ports and navigable inlets between Chesapeake Bay and the Rio Grande. But Gideon Welles, Union navy secretary, rapidly built up a force by arming almost any floating vessel until the blockade numbered some 600. Most vessels stayed close to harbors, watching for any activity. For most of the time blockade duty was dull.

Southern bases

To support the blockade, the Union navy captured bases on the Southern coast to serve as repair stations. It also captured the forts that guarded Confederate ports. The first major port to fall was the South's largest city: New Orleans, Louisiana, which fell to a Union fleet on April 25, 1862. By the end of December 1864 the only major port still open was Wilmington, North Carolina. When it was sealed off on January 15, 1865, the Confederacy lost its last link to the outside world.

Curriculum Context

What was the advantage to the North of closing the ports of the South?

Blockade-runners

Unable to construct a fleet large enough to break the blockade, the Confederacy built a few ironclad vessels, (the CSS *Virginia* and *Albemarle*). They were neither strong enough nor seaworthy enough to do the job well. A more practical tactic was to elude the blockade.

During the war about 300 vessels—privately owned, initially —tried to run the blockade. At first they were fast sailing vessels, but gradually special ships were built, many in Britain. These blockade-runners had shallow drafts to navigate small inlets and low silhouettes and gray paint to make them hard to spot. The engines burned smokeless fuels, and they had pipes to expel steam underwater to make them less visible. Above all, they were fast. Shielded by a cloudy or moonless night, a blockade-runner could sneak past patrolling warships. If that failed, it simply outran them.

The blockade's significance

Until 1863 it was Confederate policy not to sell cotton abroad in an attempt to starve European textile mills of their vital raw material. They hoped to force support from key European powers, especially Britain. The embargo failed, and the Confederacy missed the chance to export cotton when its ports were open and the Union blockade was weakest.

A photograph of the wreck of a blockade-runner on Sullivan's Island, South Carolina.

Embargo

The prevention of imports and exports from a port or country.

Even after it curtailed the embargo, the Confederate government was slow to make blockade-runners give cargo space to military supplies. Most blockade-runners operated entirely for profit, transporting luxury goods. As the war went on, the Confederacy put its own blockade-runners into service and forced private captains to set aside half their cargo space for military supplies. Right to the end of the war blockade-runners satisfied the desire of Southerners for luxury goods.

Did the blockade work?

The effectiveness of the blockade remains a matter of dispute. In 1861 blockade-runners made the trip successfully nine times out of ten, though this fell to five in ten in 1865. The blockade appears more effective when the volume of wartime shipping is compared to prewar levels. Viewed from this perspective, the blockade reduced Confederate seaborne supply by more than two-thirds.

Curriculum Context

Students may be asked to judge the relative influence on the result of the war of military, economic, social, and technological factors.

Historians also disagree about the importance of the blockade and blockade-running in the overall Union victory and Confederate defeat. Some see the blockade as the single greatest factor in the Union's triumph. Others believe that the blockade-runners were an invaluable lifeline up to the moment of Confederate defeat. A third group of historians—probably a majority—consider the blockade a significant but not decisive element in deciding the outcome of the war.

Path to Riches

Blockade-running was a lucrative business. A bale of cotton in Europe could fetch 10 times its price in the Confederacy. On the return journey captains crammed their holds with as many supplies as possible. Blockade-running captains preferred cargoes of luxury items, such as fine wines, liquor, spices, silk, coffee, and cigars, because these low-bulk, high-value items maximized their profits. The captain of a blockade-runner often earned $5,000 in gold for a successful voyage.

Costume and Dress

The Civil War had a great effect on the way civilians dressed, particularly in the Confederacy. Southern women had to use all their ingenuity to make up for fabric shortages. They made dresses from drapes, spun cotton, and made dyes.

In the mid-19th century the clothes people wore showed their social class and wealth. Working men's and women's clothes were designed for practicality and durability. Wealthy people's wardrobes were designed around the social conventions of the day.

Women's clothes

All women wore layers of clothing: undergarments, a corset, a dress with fitted bodice, and a cape. Few left the house without a bonnet to cover their hair. Wealthy women had different outfits to suit the time of day and social occasion. The fashionable costume of the day was a crinoline—a full skirt over a hooped wire frame.

Hand sewn

Women of all classes in the North and South were taught to sew, knit, and embroider. Wealthy women usually spent part of their day working on some needle art. Magazines such as *Godey's Lady's Book* and *Peterson's Magazine* published the latest styles from Paris and London for readers to either make or have made. Clothes were hand sewn until the early 1850s, when Isaac Singer's new sewing machine became widely available.

Curriculum Context

Students might be expected to describe how technological innovation altered daily life in the United States.

Children's clothes

Both boys and girls wore petticoats until the age of five. After five, boys wore either short or long trousers or knickerbockers (baggy trousers gathered below the knee). Girls' dresses were made from cotton, calico, muslin, and, in wealthier families, silk and linen. Clothes

The family of Ulysses S. Grant pictured after the war. The girl at the front wears a pinafore to keep her dress clean and a popular type of hat called a scholar, which has a ribbon hanging at the back.

were made to last, with seams that were let out as the child grew. Clothes were not washed often, so girls wore aprons or pinafores to keep their dresses clean. Zippers did not exist, so buttons fastened clothes.

Men's clothes

Fashions in men's clothes did not change as quickly as women's. Jackets and trousers were made of hard-wearing fabrics such as wool and were usually a plain dark color. Wealthy merchants and planters wore jackets of silk and linen. Men of all social classes always wore a vest and jacket. The sack coat became popular; more shapeless and looser than the formal shawl-collared jacket, it was worn by all classes. The only difference was the quality of cloth.

In New York and Boston there was a growing garment industry of ready-to-wear suits made by machine. Traditionally tailors made garments by hand. While wealthy Northern gentlemen and Southern planters continued to have custom-made clothes, the less well-off took to the new, cheaper, mass-produced garments.

Curriculum Context

This is an example of the industrialization of the North, which is often studied among the causes of the Civil War.

Wartime shortages

Before the war the South relied on the North for its manufactured cloth. The war closed off this trade, and cloth prices rose. New fabric was hard to acquire, and Southern women resorted to homespinning, dyeing, and recycling household fabric. Homespun fabric, previously only worn by black slaves and poor whites, became standard wear for all Southerners. As the war dragged on, Northern women had to make some economies but they were less severe than in the South. For a few, the wives and daughters of newly rich Northern merchants, money was plentiful, and they wore the latest fashions and fabrics. Southern women, who had been known for their style, now learned about the latest fashions from invading Union troops.

Southern ingenuity

As the war went on, the price of cloth in the South became unaffordable. In the fall of 1863 a dress that two years earlier had a price tag of $9 cost $195. In Margaret Mitchell's novel *Gone with the Wind* Southern belle Scarlett O'Hara is so desperate for fabric she

Homespun

Homespun cloth is woven from yarn made at home, usually of linen, wool, or cotton; the cloth is often looser and rougher than commercially made textiles.

Homespun Wool and Cotton

"The Southern Girl with the Homespun Dress" was a popular wartime song with lyrics that extolled female sacrifice: "My homespun dress is plain; I know my hat's quite common too; But then it shows what Southern girls for Southern rights will do."

As new cloth became more scarce, women from every social class had to make their own fabric. This meant, for the most part, homespun wool and cotton. Patriotic rich Southerners dusted off their family spinning wheels and looms and undertook the dreary task of carding and spinning wool and cotton. Poor Southerners, who had always spun their own cloth, suddenly found their skills in great demand.

Homespun, although coarse, was acceptable when used for dresses, but as undergarments and nightgowns it was very uncomfortable. One Georgia lady, Eliza Andrews, wrote in her diary, "I can stand patched-up dresses, and even take a pride in wearing Confederate homespun, where it is done open and above board, but I can't help feeling vulgar and common in coarse underclothes."

creates a gown from living-room drapes. Women from the slaveholding classes used tablecloths and bedlinen, too and made their own dyes. Toward the end of the war many Southerners were struggling to eat, let alone dress. Leather became scarcer and shoes impossible to find. Women sewed shoes out of cloth and paper, and children went barefoot. As the war went on, plantation women were sometimes forced to take back dresses they had given to their slaves.

The Civil War in the South changed women's clothing from being highly class segregated to more uniform. All women used initiative to clothe their families.

Curriculum Context

The changes in women's clothing could be seen as a visual symbol of the changes the war brought to Southern society.

The Crinoline

The crinoline, or hoop skirt, was a key fashion item for women in both the North and the South. The skirt first appeared in the 1840s. Its name came from the cotton or horsehair fabric used to make a stiff, full underskirt to hold out the skirt of the dress. In 1858 the fabric underskirt was replaced by a metal hoop frame tied at the waist.

The crinoline created a distinct shape that accentuated a woman's small waist, and it became popular with all social classes. Before the war the skirts had become increasingly full, sometimes as wide as 5 feet (1.5m) in diameter and requiring 20 yards (18m) of fabric. Only wealthy women could afford to follow the fashion to this extreme. For the working woman, who needed to move more freely, smaller hoops were more practical. In the 1860s the skirt gradually became flatter at the front and much smaller in diameter, with all the bulk at the back. It became more difficult to tell a woman's social class by the style of her dress.

One unexpected benefit of the hoop skirt during the war was its use as disguise. Some men used it to dress as women to evade enemy troops or to act as spies.

Mary Todd Lincoln, the wife of the president, pictured in 1861 wearing a fashionable full silk crinoline for a ball.

Cotton

In 1860 the South produced about 90 percent of the world's cotton. The Southern cotton crop accounted for half the exports of the United States by value, and newspapers and politicians in the South proclaimed that "Cotton is King."

The rise of cotton as the South's major crop was rapid. Despite almost perfect climatic conditions for cotton cultivation exports to Europe were small until the start of the 19th century. Cotton grown in the South was short staple. Separating the short fibers from cotton seeds to prepare the cotton for use in the textile industry was expensive and time-consuming.

The cotton gin

The problem was solved by the invention of the cotton gin in 1793. Eli Whitney mechanized the separation of cotton fibers and the seeds, allowing Southern planters to prepare the cotton crop for export efficiently. Where one person could clean the seeds from about 1 pound (0.45 kg) of cotton a day, "ginning" could clean up to 50 pounds (22.5 kg) of cotton. In 1793, before the invention of the cotton gin, just 94 tons (85 tonnes) of cotton was harvested in the United States but by 1810 the yearly total reached 45,000 tons (40,800 tonnes).

Curriculum Context

Students may be expected to understand the influence of the cotton gin on the economy in the South.

Cotton and the conflict

Cotton was mainly produced by Southern planters who used slave labor as free white labor was too expensive. The boom in cotton production brought a sharp rise in slave numbers. In 1790 there were around 657,000 slaves in the Southern states. By 1860 there were 3.5 million slaves in the South.

Curriculum Context

It might be interesting to understand the economic factors that underlay slavery in the South.

Growing cotton depleted the soil, so new land for cotton production was sought in the West. As cotton production spread, so did the slave economy into

The interior of a building housing a cotton gin. The invention of the gin led to a boom in cotton production at the beginning of the 19th century.

Curriculum Context

Some curricula ask students to understand how slavery became an important issue due to the country's westward expansion.

Spindle

A device for spinning yarn from fibers, either by hand or as part of a spinning machine.

regions that had been worked by free labor. The expansion of slavery into new areas created dangerous tension between North and South. The cotton boom meant that the emancipation question became an issue of expansion both in terms of slave numbers and territory. The extent to which cotton was behind the South's secession was illustrated by Alabama's state flag (adopted in January 1861), which pictured a cotton plant with a rattlesnake around it. The motto read *Noli Me Tangere*, meaning "Touch Me Not."

Cotton as a weapon

Confederate politicians saw the cotton crop as key in their struggle against the Union and hoped to damage the Union economy. By July 1862 around a quarter of the North's spindles were still operational, and costs were mounting as the price of raw cotton spiraled. Cotton was grown within the Union, and in Illinois met with moderate success. But quantities were negligible and Northern textile mills were largely closed down.

Despite the high prices cotton reached in the North, Confederate patriots were keen to keep it from the Union. Some 2.5 million bales of cotton were burned as Union troops advanced.

Cotton diplomacy

Cotton was also seen by the South as a vital tool to gain international recognition of the Confederacy. From 1861 the Southern planters initiated a voluntary but widespread embargo against shipments to Europe.

Deprived of their markets, many Southern planters also planted corn—it became seen as a patriotic duty to grow food rather than cash crops. The cotton crop of 1861 yielded 4.5 million bales of cotton. In 1863 the South produced fewer than half a million bales.

Misguided policy

Southern diplomatic logic was flawed. Bumper cotton crops in 1859 and 1860 meant that by 1861 European mills were overstocked with raw cotton and unsold finished products, so the export embargo initially had little effect. It was not until 1863 that England's Lancashire mill workers went onto short-time working. By then the Union blockade of the Southern coast was so effective that exports were difficult, even though a cash-strapped Confederacy was anxious to exchange cotton for military supplies in Europe. In fact, it was the export of cotton through the cotton bonds scheme that allowed the Confederacy to finance much of its military effort in the later years of the war.

Curriculum Context

How might it have changed the war if the South had gained international recognition?

Confederate Cotton Bonds

In 1863 the Confederate government struck a deal with the French banking house of Emile Erlanger & Company. The bank agreed to sell $15 million worth of Confederate bonds (paper money) to private investors. The so-called Erlanger loan was unusual because the bonds were guaranteed not by gold but by "white gold"—cotton. Investors could exchange the bonds for cotton after the war at a good rate. The loan was hugely popular, attracting a host of high-profile investors in England, including the future prime minister, William Ewart Gladstone. The Confederate government used the money to buy vitally needed armaments and supplies for the troops.

Daily Life

In the United States in the 1860s, where people lived, and whether they were male or female, black or white, had a huge effect on their daily life. There were many differences in the way of life and outlook between the regions.

Curriculum Context

Do you think that stereotypes are still based on geographical regions today?

Where people lived had the greatest effect on their lives. By 1860 stereotypes abounded of shrewd and businesslike Northerners, gracious and dashing Southerners, and crude but honest Westerners. "Yankee" was shorthand for a Northerner who lived above the Mason–Dixon line that divided Pennsylvania from Maryland. They were thought more educated, literate, and business-oriented than the rest of the country but also practical and money-grasping.

Life in the North

Most of the 22 million people in the North still lived in rural areas, and lived according to the rhythm of the seasons. But increasingly people lived in cities and towns with more than 20,000 inhabitants. Literacy was an important business skill. A public education system had started in many states in the 1830s. Boys went to school in the day; girls went very early in the morning (5:00 A.M. to 7:00 A.M.) and late in the afternoon (4:00 P.M. to 6:00 P.M.), if they went at all. Many parents were willing to send their sons to school, but felt there was little point educating girls beyond the basics of reading, writing, and math, since most girls would marry and stay in the home.

Curriculum Context

Some curricula ask students to be able to trace the development of public schools in the United States.

In urban areas a child from a well-off family might go to school all day, come home and play or help with chores around the house, read, play music, listen to stories, have a bath on Saturday nights, go to church on Sundays, and in many ways, live a life recognizable to 21st-century children.

Life in the country

In rural areas life was much harder. There were few if any schools, although when the government sold land to settlers in Northern states, part of the money had to be set aside to fund a public education system. Most children were taught to read and write by their parents. There was little time for learning, as most of the day was taken up with farmwork starting at dawn.

Northern cities

Cities were noisy, dirty, smelly places. Sewer systems were rare. Buildings also became more crowded since immigrants from Europe, particularly Germany and Ireland, often lived one family to a room while trying to establish themselves in their new lives.

Education in the South

More people were able to read and write in the North than the South. The distances between settlements in the rural South meant public education was rare. Southern farmers might send their sons to schools at a local plantation whose owner had a tutor for his own children. Students would spend the day or week on lessons, then return home to work on the weekends.

Curriculum Context

It might be interesting to consider why so many immigrants headed for Northern cities rather than the South.

Life in Factories

Many jobs in urban areas were in factories, as developments and inventions enabled Northerners to become less dependent on imports from Europe. Factory workers faced a long day. Most were used to responding to the bell and the clock instead of the sun, since factories had been around since the late 1790s, and third and fourth generations of American workers were now used to manufacturing cloth, stovepipes, railroad engines, and a thousand other items.

There were few unions or labor organizations to protect workers from wage cuts and dangerous working conditions. Workers could be fired for joining a union. The workday began before dawn and ended 12 to 14 hours later, with half days on Saturday. Employers often hired boys and girls instead of adults to save on wages, so urban children, particularly children of newly arrived immigrants who did not know how the education system worked, might never go to school.

Upper class boys and girls were educated in this way, with boys learning subjects such as philosophy, theology, and mathematics, and girls sewing, painting, and other fine arts. Poorer children rarely received an education, since they worked all day on the farm. Black children, too, were rarely educated; by 1860 it was illegal to teach slaves to read and write in case they rebelled against slavery.

Southern slavery

The existence of slavery in the South was the biggest difference between life in the North and South. In the North, states outlawed slavery beginning in the 18th century; but slavery in the South not only lasted, it was encouraged by the spread of cotton. The lucrative crop was so labor intensive many farmers believed that they could not survive without slave labor to do the work.

If you were black and lived in the South, you were probably a slave. There were some free blacks, who might be artisans, laundresses, or ministers in a particular town. They had to carry papers at all times proving they were free or risk arrest or even reenslavement. Only a few Southerners were slave-holders; but since they were the richest and most powerful people, who owned businesses and ran the political system, slavery touched all aspects of daily life.

Life in the South

Large plantation owners oversaw the work of hundreds of slaves. Plantation owners' wives often had large numbers of house slaves to manage, as well as families to feed and clothe. Many owners had other businesses and when they traveled, they left the plantation to their wives, who were known as plantation mistresses.

Like Northern women, Southern women were in charge of the home and family. Black and white children played together, until black children were

Curriculum Context

If curricula examine the differences between the North and the South before the war, slavery is one of the most important points to consider.

Labor intensive

Requiring many people to do certain work.

considered old enough to work, usually between the ages of four and seven. They mostly worked in the fields alongside their parents, but some were taught a trade or craft and put to work as an apprentice to a skilled worker. Others became house servants. As fears of slave uprisings increased, slaves and free blacks were restricted more and more in their daily activities. For example, meeting in groups, even in church, without white supervision was frowned on or banned outright.

A slave family outside a house in Hampton, Virginia, in 1861. In the South the daily life of both slaves and free blacks was strictly regulated, since Southern whites had a great fear of rebellion.

Rigid society

Both black and white children were taught early on to be aware of their place in society. Black children had to be careful how they talked to whites, lest they be considered rude, for which they could be beaten or arrested. White children were taught that blacks were inferior and benefited from slavery, which gave them Christianity and "civilized" them. Much of what people learned reinforced the existing social structure.

Western pioneers

In the West people had more social mobility than the North or South. Many Americans thought Westerners crude and unrefined. Many were, but daily life on the frontier was so difficult they had little patience for people who thought birth gave them special privileges. The battle against nature was a great equalizer.

Curriculum Context

The nature of the frontier society that developed in the West features in many curricula.

Curriculum Context

It may be useful to compare the treatment of Native Americans with the positions the major groups took at the outbreak of the Civil War.

In 1860 most Westerners were farmers. They settled on land taken from Native Americans who, angered by the invasion, fought back. By the 1860s, however, many Native Americans had been pushed so far west that fewer attacks occurred.

Hard life

Farming Western soil was difficult. Prairie grasses grew more than 6 feet (1.8m) tall with deep roots. A steel-bladed plow, developed by John Deere in 1837, meant farmers could turn the soil and plant crops. As farmers settled lands, small towns spread very slowly with neighbors often far away. Life was lonely, especially for women used to having family close by back east. Daily life was a grind. Western women did the same chores as other women, but without modern conveniences such as a cook stove (the first portable one was patented around 1850), or a sewing machine (invented in 1846), or even a hand pump to get water from the well. The weather was fierce, with tornadoes, blizzards, prairie fires, constant wind, and scorching summer heat. The traditional divisions of labor between men and women did not survive in such a demanding world. Both men and women worked as needed.

Curriculum Context

Students may be asked to consider the status of pioneer women and their role in settling and developing the West.

Stereotypes

Each region was also home to people whose lives differed from the norm: Both black and white children sometimes got a good education; some women worked in business and politics, some Southern men were in business, while some Northern men were gentlemen of leisure, and there were Westerners as cultured and genteel as Europeans. For the majority of people where they lived determined how people saw them. Their ethnic background determined if they were free or slave, educated or not, poor or not. Their gender shaped their daily activities and how involved in the larger world they became. In the 19th century, all these factors determined their daily lives.

Genteel

Elegant and graceful, as if from the upper classes.

Economy of the North

The Northern states had an industrialized economy based on manufacturing and selling a wide range of goods. The North had a more diverse economy than the South and was better able to finance the war and to supply its army.

In nearly every respect the Northern states had a formidable economic advantage over the South. In 1860 the North's population of 22 million was more than twice that of the South, including the South's 3.5 million slaves. The North had more than 110,000 factories, the South just 18,000. The North produced 94 percent of the country's iron, 97 percent of its coal, and 97 percent of its firearms. It owned 90 percent of the country's merchant ship tonnage and had 22,000 miles (35,200 km) of railroad, compared with just under 9,000 miles (14,400 km) in the South. Pennsylvania and New York each had more industry than the entire South. Northerners held 75 percent of the farm acreage, produced 60 percent of its livestock, 67 percent of its corn, and 81 percent of its wheat. Northerners held 75 percent of the nation's total taxable wealth.

Curriculum Context

The industrialization of the North is key to any understanding of U.S. history in the 19th century.

Prewar finance

The conventional wisdom of wartime finance in the mid-19th century was that governments should only meet normal expenses through taxation and pay for the war largely through borrowing. The prewar United States also had a tradition of low taxes. Aside from a few internal taxes, for example on tobacco, the population had been free of direct federal taxation for over 40 years. Although everyone knew the war would require some change, most people underestimated the financial measures that would be required. The government had used traditional policies to finance the War of 1812 and the Mexican War (1846–1848), albeit with limited success.

A Nation Divided

The difference between how the Northern and Southern states made money was at the heart of the political conflict that led to war. The Northern states' economy was based on manufacturing such as textile mills and factories. In general, Northerners approved of tariffs (taxes on foreign goods) because they made imported goods more expensive, encouraging people to buy Northern-made items.

Northern manufacturers and entrepreneurs invested in roads, canals, and railroads to transport their goods from place to place to sell.

Northern people saw progress in terms of industry, invention, and transportation.

While a few prewar voices in the South advocated that business embrace manufacturing and industry, the South's economy remained based on agriculture, particularly cash crops to export. The South relied on manufactured goods from the North and abroad, and so supported low tariffs. Plantation owners could make huge profits, particularly from cotton after the invention of the gin in the 1790s. They invested their profits in more land and slaves to work it.

Curriculum Context

It may be interesting to consider why the Confederacy did not change its financial approach sooner, and what alternatives were available.

Financial trouble

Both the Union and the Confederacy began the Civil War with traditional financial policies. The Confederacy did not alter its approach and by midwar found itself in financial trouble, with a lack of specie (hard currency), especially gold, and runaway inflation. The Union government could have gone down a similar path. Initially, it did. By New Year's Day 1862 the government had run out of money. The Secretary of the Treasury Salmon P. Chase told President Lincoln there was no more money and that he could not think of any other ways to raise more.

Financial revolution

While Chase lacked fresh ideas, others did not. An exceptional group of businessmen, bankers, and attorneys stepped forward with advice, and both Congress and Chase listened to them. The result was "a fiscal-military revolution" according to one historian. The Union managed to direct its economy to pay for the war by using a mixture of loans, paper money, and internal taxes.

Fiscal
Relating to taxation and government revenues.

By the Legal Tender Act of February 1862 the government issued $150 million in Treasury notes, (greenbacks). These notes were not directly backed by gold reserves. People had to accept the notes for all debts, public or private, with two exceptions: customs duties and interest on government bonds. The system made government bonds a very attractive investment. The bonds sold briskly, and not just to banks and wealthy investors. Ordinary citizens could buy bonds in notes as low as $50, and a large-scale advertising campaign worked overtime to make sure that they did.

Higher taxes

Even with government bonds selling well, the payment of war expenses required further issues of paper money: $450 million by early 1863. A National Banking Act, passed in April of that year, helped regulate the currency, but wartime inflation had, eventually, to be remedied with taxation. The Internal Revenue Act of July 1862 placed a tax on the income of those earning more than $600 a year and also brought in a series of internal taxes on goods.

Bonds

Bonds are a form of saving in which an investor buys certificates that can be cashed in later at an attractive rate of interest.

Curriculum Context

The financial legislation passed during the Civil War helped shape modern finance in the United States.

Wartime Profits

War boosted demand for certain products, and businessmen seized the chance to make money. In general, only the already wealthy were able to take advantage. With federal arsenals and shipyards overloaded, the government turned to private arms manufacturers and shipping tycoons. At the outbreak of war Cornelius Vanderbilt, who owned a large steamship business, sold most of his ships to the Union navy. After further investments in railroads, he built a fortune of $105,000,000 and became the richest man in the world. Andrew Carnegie invested $11,000 in an oil company in Titusville, Pennsylvania, in 1861 and received a return of $17,868 after only one year. Meanwhile Philip Armour began his Chicago meat-packing empire by selling pork to the Union army.

Some prewar inventions brought vast rewards in wartime. Gail Borden (1801–1874) patented the condensed-milk process in 1856 but saw the collapse of two successive milk-condensing plants in 1856 and 1857. During the war, long-lasting milk became essential to the diets of many Union soldiers, and Borden made a fortune.

Tax revenue helped the United States government pay for the war effort without ruinous inflation. By the end of the Civil War prices in the Union stood just 80 percent above their levels in 1861. In the Confederacy prices had increased 100 percent by mid 1862, and inflation rose to 9,000 percent before the end of the war. But life in the North during the war years was not easy. Inflation cut real wages among industrial laborers by about 20 percent, which provoked unrest, strikes, and even riots.

Effects of the Union's financial policy

The North's innovative financial policy permanently changed the national economy. It set up a uniform national currency, issued and regulated by the federal government. The system also translated the North's edge in manufacturing, agriculture, and transportation into goods and services that could support the vast Union armies. The war cost the North about $2.3 billion, representing spending equivalent to 70 percent of the 1859 gross national product.

War boom

The war created opportunities for profit in some areas of industry, manufacture, investment, and enterprise. The loss of Southern cotton led to a wartime decline in Northern production of cotton textiles (the North's largest prewar industry), but boosted the manufacture of woolens. Supplying the army boosted the North's shoe and leather industries. War-related industries invariably prospered, especially the manufacture of weapons, gunpowder, and wagons. The coal and iron industries grew during the war, stimulating further industrial growth.

Encouraging enterprise

The Homestead Act of 1862 was the first law to encourage enterprise. It granted a farmer 160 acres of federal land in the West after they had lived on the land for five years and improved it. A total of 80 million acres were allocated in this way, and the Homestead Act gave a major push to western migration. Congress also passed the Morrill Land-Grant College Act, which gave each state territory in order to establish colleges to train farmers and mechanics. About 25 million acres were allocated in this fashion. Many universities can trace their origins to the Morrill Act. Finally, Congress passed the Pacific Railroad Act, giving several railroad companies 120 million acres of land in the West to build transcontinental railroads. The result was an extension of the eastern economy into the West and the creation of a truly national economy.

Creating an industrial giant

The government's wartime economic measures created what one historian has called a "blueprint for modern America." But for these measures, the postwar United States would not have emerged in the way it did. Although historians disagree about whether the war hindered or accelerated industrialization in America, they agree that it shifted the economic balance of power from agriculture to manufacturing.

Mechanics
Mechanics are strictly any workers who work with their hands, but the modern word usually refers to people who repair machines.

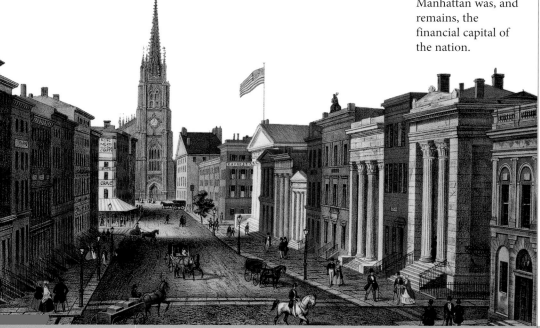

Wall Street, New York, in 1847. This narrow street in Manhattan was, and remains, the financial capital of the nation.

Economy of the South

A unique economic system developed in the Southern states in the decades before the Civil War. Wealthy Southerners put nearly all their money into land and slaves to grow cash crops to sell to the North and abroad.

Although the South amassed great wealth between 1800 and 1860, its economy was fragile for three major reasons. First, Southern farmers relied on only a few major cash crops, namely cotton, tobacco, and sugar. Second, profits were falsely high because they relied on unpaid slave labor. Last, with money rolling in from the sale of cotton, many Southerners saw no need to develop manufacturing and industry. The cracks in this prosperous economy were pushed open by the war.

The rise of plantations

The plantation system of slave-based farming was well established in the South in the 1700s. Then, cotton was grown only in a few coastal areas of Georgia and South Carolina. This changed in the 1790s, with the invention of the cotton gin making it possible to efficiently separate cotton seeds from the fluffy cotton fiber. By the early 1800s factories for weaving cotton cloth were being built in Britain and the northeastern United States, creating demand for Southern cotton.

In the 1800s the new states of Alabama, Mississippi, Louisiana, and eventually Texas were opened up to white settlement. The warm climate and rich soil of these states were perfect for growing cotton. Planters began moving from the older Southern states into these new states, taking their slaves with them and establishing cotton plantations. Between 1810 and 1820 the combined population of Mississippi and Alabama increased fivefold, from 40,500 to 222,500.

Curriculum Context

The changes brought by the cotton gin are key to understanding the development of the Southern economy in the early 19th century.

Curriculum Context

The role of landscape and climate in shaping U.S. history features in some curricula.

A slave economy

Slavery made it possible to profitably grow other cash crops. Planters also grew tobacco and rice in the eastern states of the South. Hemp production spread into the upper Southern states of Kentucky, Tennessee, and Missouri. It was used to make ropes and sacking. In southern Louisiana sugar cane became an important crop. Large-scale planters also grew corn and raised hogs and cattle for food. But many found cotton so profitable they wanted to use all of their slaves in the cotton fields. They often bought corn and meat from local farmers, so that even nonslaveholders became dependent on the planters for some of their income.

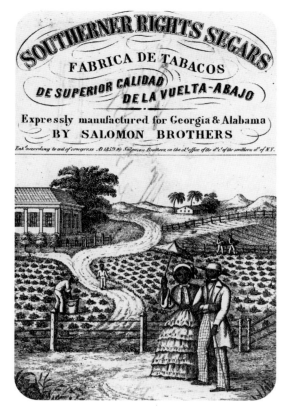

A label for cigars manufactured by a New York company from Southern tobacco. The label shows a highly idealized view of slave life on a tobacco plantation in the South.

North versus South

On the eve of the war Southern cotton made up three-quarters of the world supply. Many Southerners believed that the industrial economies of the North and Europe could not survive without Southern cotton for their textile industries. In 1857 South Carolina's James Henry Hammond addressed the U.S. Senate, "No, you do not dare make war on cotton. No power on earth dares make war on it. Cotton is king."

Detractors in the North pointed to the lack of economic development and diversity in the South. The South was undoubtedly at a severe disadvantage to the North in a number of areas critical to the conflict. In 1860 the North had nearly 90 percent of the nation's manufacturing capacity and two-thirds of its railroad

Detractors
People who diminish the importance or value of something.

tracks. It produced 15 times as much iron as the South and 24 times as many locomotives. The Confederacy had only one factory capable of casting large cannons, the Tredegar Iron Works in Richmond, Virginia. While this did not make a Southern defeat inevitable, it made it hard for the Confederacy to compete with the Union.

Withholding cotton

Soon after the start of war President Jefferson Davis gambled on the Confederacy's greatest asset. He secretly encouraged planters not to sell cotton to Britain and the rest of Europe, hoping Britain would then recognize the Confederacy as an independent nation and perhaps side with them. But Britain had begun to develop its own cotton sources in Egypt and India. So even though its economy was affected by the Confederacy's actions, its textile industry survived. The South's economy, however, was severely damaged. Unsold cotton piled up, and the Confederacy found it difficult to pay for the war without its chief source of income. In border states, and areas where Union armies invaded, some planters even sold cotton to the enemy.

By the time the Confederate government reversed its policy of withholding cotton in 1863, it was too late. The Union blockade of the Southern coastline meant Union ships patrolling the coast stopped crops from being exported and much-needed supplies from getting in. During the first year of the war the blockade was not effective, but by the war's end a blockading fleet of 700 ships was strangling Confederate trade.

Paying for the war

The Confederate government had three financial means to pay for the war: taxation, loans, and printing money. Taxation was strongly opposed across the Confederacy. The Confederate Congress gingerly enacted its first two taxes in 1861 with little success. The first brought in only $3.5 million during the whole

Curriculum Context

The cotton industry of the British Empire is a good example of the sometimes unexpected ways in which world events are interconnected with a domestic event such as the Civil War.

Blockade

Using ships or soldiers to prevent people or supplies from reaching an enemy country or port.

Towns of the South

There were towns and cities in the Old South, but they existed mainly to support the agricultural economy. Smaller towns usually had gins, which cleaned and packed cotton into large bales for shipping. Farmers could purchase supplies and equipment for their farms in local stores. In places like Atlanta, Mobile, New Orleans, and Memphis businessmen bought and stored cotton and other crops before shipping them to markets in the North or in Europe. Mills were built to extract oil from the cotton seeds. Baltimore and Richmond were major flour-milling centers. Doctors and lawyers practiced their professions in Southern cities. Compared to the North or to Europe, however, Southern cities remained small. In 1860 only 7 percent of Southerners lived in towns with a population greater than 2,500 people. Five Southern states had no city with 10,000 citizens. New Orleans was the largest Southern city before the Civil War, but with a population of 170,000 it was still small compared with Northern cities such as New York, which had well over a million people. New Orleans was nearly four times the size of the next-largest Southern city, which was Charleston, South Carolina. In fact, the percentage of Southerners living in urban areas actually declined between 1840 and 1860, which indicates the importance of agriculture—and especially cotton—to the South's economic system. Slavery was the foundation of that economy.

war. The second was a tax of 0.5 percent on property. The central government relied on individual states to collect taxes, and many state governments were obstructive. For example, Texas tried to pay its taxes by printing its own state notes. The Confederacy only raised between 5 and 6 percent of its funds by taxation. The Union raised 21 percent in this way.

The Confederacy raised approximately $34 million by guaranteeing lenders a good price on cotton after the war. The government relied most heavily on printing paper money. In May 1861 congress approved the printing of $20 million in treasury notes. Unlike the Union, it did not compel acceptance of the notes by law. In total the Confederacy printed $1.5 billion in bank notes during the war. They began losing value from the moment they were printed. By the beginning of 1863 it took seven dollars to buy what a dollar had bought two years earlier. Near the end of the war

Curriculum Context

How did the Confederacy's need to raise taxes compare with its support for states' rights, one of its main reasons for going to war?

inflation in the Confederacy was so high (about 9,000 percent) paper money was almost worthless and most goods could only be bought with gold or by barter.

Hardship

By 1863 Southerners were suffering severe hardship. The absence of adult men on Southern farms had reduced crop yields. Almost constant warfare had destroyed fertile farmland in Virginia and Tennessee. The Confederate army comandeered food for soldiers and took over railroads, interrupting the transportation of goods. There were shortages of the most basic goods such as sugar, flour, and salt. Bread riots broke out in Richmond, Virginia in April.

Devastation

As the Union army penetrated deeper, slaves fled by the thousands to Union lines, depriving the South of labor. In fall 1864 Union General William T. Sherman's army marched through Georgia destroying everything they could not eat; they burned fields, houses, cotton, and gins, and melted and twisted the railroads.

Despite the devastation the South achieved economic recovery within a decade. By 1871 the South was exporting even more cotton than it had before the war.

Branding cattle on the prairies of Texas. The South had an economy based largely on agriculture, which was a great disadvantage in the Civil War.

Family Life

The conflict sometimes known as "the Brothers' War" affected most American families and tore many apart, setting relatives against each other as some supported the Union while others were drawn to the Confederate cause.

The Civil War had a unique and lasting impact on family life and was the catalyst for profound changes in the role of women in North American society. The Civil War was unlike any other conflict in U.S. history. It was fought so close to home noncombatants became caught up in the action as never before. During the Civil War American men fought each other in the very fields and orchards in which they had played with their own parents and children. Many centers of civilian population were so near the front line that private homes were pressed into service as temporary supply bases or even military headquarters; churches and schoolhouses were turned into makeshift hospitals and morgues. The civilian population helped care for the sick and wounded. Yet family life—or at least a version of it—went on despite the carnage.

Makeshift

A word describing a temporary and often crude arrangement.

Women's changing role

The mass exodus of men to the battlefields changed women's role in the family. In the mid-19th century American women's lives were based around home and family, while the world of business and public life was the preserve of men. Only 25 percent of white women worked outside the home before they were married and only 5 percent after they were married.

Curriculum Context

The impact of the Civil War on women's lives is highlighted in virtually all history curricula.

At the start of the conflict women used traditional skills to support the men who were close enough to their own or their comrades' homes to drop back when necessary. Women sewed uniforms, prepared food, and treated minor injuries. When the men returned to the battlefront, their male children below the age of enlistment took on some of their daily responsibilities, such as chopping wood and mending fences.

On the home front in the South many towns came to be inhabited exclusively by white women, children, and slaves. As the war went on, women took on more responsibilities for which they had little or no practical experience. In addition to their work in the home they took charge of their husbands' farms and businesses. They became farmers, plantation managers, clerks, and munitions-plant workers. Many taught school. In North Carolina only 7 percent of teachers were women in 1860. By the end of the war women made up more than half the staff of the state's schools. Once women found they were capable of doing work previously considered "men's work," they gained new confidence.

Divided families

Like all wars, the Civil War broke up families through death. There was hardly a family in the South that did not lose a son, brother, or father. The conflict also divided families in other ways, and breakups could be almost as painful as bereavement. Not every family was united in its support for one side or the other. President Lincoln himself was affected: His wife's four brothers fought for the Confederates. One of them was killed.

Curriculum Context

Do you think that the changes introduced by the Civil War still have an influence in the public education system today?

Bereavement

The loss of a loved one through death.

An etching of a painting by Trevor McClurg, 1866. A wounded soldier is welcomed home after the Civil War. Family life was profoundly affected by the war, both because of its long duration and because it was fought around people's homes.

Slave Families

Many slaves married and raised families, even though marriages between slaves were not recognized by law. Slave-owners often encouraged slaves to form families, partly because they relied on childbirth to add to slave numbers, especially after an 1807 law banned the importation of new slaves from Africa. Slave-owners also believed that if slaves married and settled down, they were less likely to be rebellious or to run away.

While responsible slave-owners respected slave families, others destroyed them by either selling or relocating one or more family members. As many as one in four slave families were broken up in this way. Abolitionists often highlighted this to gain support for their cause. For example, the emotional power of Harriet Beecher Stowe's abolitionist novel *Uncle Tom's Cabin* (1852) comes from her harrowing depiction of the suffering caused by slavery's effect on family relationships.

Conflicting loyalties

Confederate General Robert E. Lee also had conflicting loyalties and had to chose between his conscience and family ties. When he was offered command of the Union forces, Lee replied that although he failed to see the good of secession, he could not go against his native Virginia. As he put it: "I could not raise my hand against my birthplace, my home, my children." Lee resigned his commission and later took command of the Army of Northern Virginia, which became the most famous of the Confederate armies. Many others were in the same predicament. Flora Cook, the daughter of General St. George Cook of the Union army, was married to J.E.B. ("Jeb") Stuart, who gave up his commission in the U.S. army to join the Confederacy. Jeb asked Flora to move with their children south of the Mason–Dixon line. Although it appalled her Unionist family, Flora resettled in Saltville, Virginia.

Dilemmas such as these were commonplace. The Civil War damaged the family not just by depriving it forever of one or more of its family members, but also by causing crises of conscience and principle that were impossible to resolve without pain.

> **Curriculum Context**
>
> When studying the motivation of key individuals such as Robert E. Lee, remember to consider personal and family commitments as much as political ideals.

Food

In 1860 the United States was largely a farm economy that produced enough food to support its entire population. During the Civil War the North was able to feed its citizens, but the South suffered badly from shortages and high prices.

In both the Confederate and Union armies a soldier's basic food rations included hardbread, beef, beans, and coffee. Union rations varied little throughout the war, but Southern rations were reduced as the war went on.

The staple of all troops was hardbread. Known as hardtack, ship's biscuit, teeth-dullers, or pilot bread, this was a dry crackerlike biscuit made from flour, salt, and water. In the South it was often made from cornmeal. It did not spoil easily and was fairly nutritious. The bread was made at government bakeries and shipped in barrels. By the time it reached army camps, it was rock hard and sometimes had to be broken with a rifle butt. The soldiers made it more edible by soaking it in coffee or soup or frying it in bacon grease. Weevils often infested it and soldiers joked that the bugs were their main source of meat.

Although beef was a staple, it was not always available. Herds of cattle sometimes went along with troops and were slaughtered as required. Otherwise, troops ate salted beef or pork. Frequently the meat was old or spoiled, and many soldiers became sick or even died from eating bad meat. The beans were dried white navy beans that needed soaking overnight and then cooking for hours before they were edible. They had little flavor but added bulk to meals and were cheap.

Coffee had become popular shortly before the war and was the most important drink for a soldier. The North bought the best possible coffee for its troops. In the

Staple
The main part of a diet.

Curriculum Context

Telling details help explain the experience of the war for ordinary soldiers.

Salted beef

Fresh meat was often salted in order to preserve it.

South, however, the Union blockade meant coffee was hard to come by. Southerners had to buy whatever they could or make do with a poor coffee substitute, such as acorn coffee.

Other rations

While in camp each Union soldier was issued with the following daily rations: 12 oz. (0.3 kg) pork or bacon, or 1 lb. 4 oz. (0.56 kg) fresh or salt beef; 1 lb. 6 oz. (0.62 kg) soft bread or flour, or 1 lb. (0.45 kg) hardbread, or 1 lb. 4 oz. (0.56 kg) cornmeal. For every 100 men there was also 15 lb. (6.8 kg) beans or peas and 10 lb. (4.5 kg) rice or hominy; 10 lb. (4.5 kg) green coffee or 8 lb. (3.6 kg) roasted coffee; 1 lb. 8 oz. (0.68 kg) tea; 15 lb. (6.8 kg) sugar; 4 quarts (3.8 l) vinegar; 1 quart (0.9 l) molasses. The Confederate army adopted the same ration at the start of the war, but later reduced it due to food shortages and distribution problems. Troops supplemented their rations by various means. Their families might send them food parcels, or they bought

Curriculum Context

It might be interesting to compare the daily ration with what you and your family eat in a day.

Starving Troops

An officer in the Confederate Army of Northern Virginia described the soldiers' food situation in spring 1865:

"There was no fear in the Confederate ranks of any thing that General Grant might do; but there was an appalling and well-founded fear of starvation, which indeed some of us were already suffering. From the beginning of that campaign our food supply had been barely sufficient to sustain life, and on the march from Spotsylvania to Cold Harbor it would have been a gross exaggeration to describe it in that way. In my own battery three hard biscuits and one very meager slice of fat pork were issued to each man on our arrival, and that was the first food any of us had seen since our halt two days before. The next supply did not come til two days later, and it consisted of a single cracker per man, with no meat at all. We hoarded what we had, allowing ourselves only a nibble at any one time, and that only when the pangs of hunger became unbearable.

"But what is the use of writing about the pangs of hunger? The words are utterly meaningless to persons who have never known actual starvation. . . . It is a horror, which once suffered, leaves an impression which is never erased from the memory."

A company kitchen in a Union army camp, 1864. There were no trained cooks and little equipment. Soldiers usually prepared and ate their food in a small group, or mess, of about five people.

Curriculum Context

Before Lincoln's proclamation there had been no standard national holiday; states had celebrated Thanksgiving when they chose.

food from sutlers. These licensed traders followed troops to sell them foods such as pickles, cheese, sardines, cakes, and candies, as well as beer and whiskey, even though troops were forbidden to drink alcohol. Sutlers' food was often prepared in unhygienic conditions and made soldiers sick. Army commanders on both sides also led foraging expeditions to find extra provisions.

Thanksgiving feast

In October 1863 President Lincoln proclaimed that Thanksgiving should be celebrated on the last Thursday in November. For Thanksgiving 1864 the Union public gave their soldiers a Thanksgiving feast. Everyone sent what they could: turkeys or ham or beef. Oysters were a highlight. Other donations, such as gingerbread, cakes, pickles, apples, cheese, and mince pies, were all a welcome change from normal rations.

Southern home front

From the summer of 1861 prices rose dramatically and from 1862 food shortages started to be felt across the Confederacy. By 1863 many Southerners had become desperate for even basic foodstuffs, and people grew used to going hungry. In April a mob, mainly of women, rioted in the Confederate capital, Richmond, Virginia, demanding the government distribute bread.

By early 1863 meat had virtually disappeared from the daily diet throughout the South. Many families lived on a diet of cornbread with sorghum, field peas, and milk. Every social class ate cornbread. One plantation family in North Louisiana lived on cornbread, butter, and milk until mid-1863, when their diet was reduced to sugar and flour. Other plantation families lived off vegetables and fruit they grew. Inflation meant that by mid-1863 a bushel of corn cost $50 or more. For those living close to the front lines or in towns, prices were higher.

Inflation
A rapid and widespread rise in prices.

Coffee shortage

As coffee became harder to find in the South, people tried out substitutes, including corn, wheat, sweet potatoes, okra, and even cotton. None of them tasted anything like coffee. One possible source of coffee beans was Northern peddlers who traveled to the South with wagons laden with supplies, but many Southerners resisted buying from the enemy. As inflation gripped the South, many could not afford the prices anyway.

Peddler
A merchant who sells his goods by traveling around or by going door to door.

Differences in the North and South

Although food was grown across the South until late into the war, it became harder to find laborers to plant and harvest the crops. The breakdown of the South's transportation network meant food could not be distributed. The Union's industrial strength meant it could use the recently invented tin can to preserve food. The Union government issued troops with new products such as condensed milk.

Curriculum Context

If you are asked to discuss technological innovation during the Civil War, bear in mind that it did not only include weapons.

The availability and price of food during the Civil War reflected the different fortunes of the North and South. The North carried on much as before. Some men in the army had never eaten so well. In the South both civilians and, later, troops found their diets restricted. Toward the end of the war many were hungry. Women and children were malnourished and underweight.

Home Front, Confederate

Southern civilians experienced the war in a much more immediate way than their Northern counterparts. The war was fought largely on Southern territory, on their doorsteps, even in their very homes, forever altering Southern lives.

Curriculum Context

The experiences of people on the home front are studied in all national history curricula.

In 1861 most Southerners welcomed the war with enthusiasm, thinking the war would be short and the North quickly defeated. With three out of four eligible men serving in the Confederate army the Southern home front was a world of women, children, and slaves. As their men marched off to war, Confederate women threw themselves into activities such as sewing flags, raising money, and organizing hospitals and relief associations.

Support for the cause

White Southerners of the elite planter class had an unwavering faith in the Confederate cause, which they maintained until the end of the war. They thought their own interests represented those of all Southerners. Many did not even consider that slaves might have a different stake in the outcome—or that there might be differences of opinion among whites. When some poorer white men showed reluctance to join the army, planter families concluded that it was a result of personal cowardice rather than political belief.

Curriculum Context

How much do you think everyone in the South shared the same view of the aims of the war?

Women as managers

Women often had to take charge of family farms when the men were away fighting, and plantation owners' wives had to run the plantations. Their husbands wrote letters full of agricultural advice from planting to managing the slaves but the mail service was irregular, and effectively women were on their own. Some rose to the occasion, while others crumbled under increasing pressure.

Of all plantation duties it was usually slave management that planter-class women found most challenging. Mistresses did not command the same authority as masters. Slaves began to leave work undone, ignore orders, or run away to the Union lines. Many planter women could not, or would not, accept that slavery was ending and clung to the belief that slaves really were passive, faithful, and helpless.

The "Twenty Negro" Law

Early in the war the Confederate authorities were sympathetic to the problems of unsupervised slaves. A law, allowing any plantation with more than 20 slaves to have a white man (a master or overseer) exempted from duty as a soldier was passed. Poorer families saw this law as favoring the upper classes, especially as they struggled to provide for their own hungry families.

Overseer
A supervisor employed to manage workers.

Southern shortages

The strain on Southern agriculture was huge. Despite the conversion of thousands of acres of cotton to staple crops, by 1862 food shortages were severe. The problem was often the lack of any organized distribution system. Military shipments took priority on

Bread Riots

Despite the Confederate government's best efforts, increasing desperation led to civilian protests across the South. By the spring of 1863 the last crops from the previous year's drought-ravaged season were running out. Prices spiraled out of control. A family's weekly grocery bill for staples such as flour and butter had risen from a prewar $6.55 to $68.25. Civilians thought that storekeepers and the government were hoarding supplies, and starving women staged bread riots.

The worst of these riots occurred in Richmond, Virginia, where several hundred women—later joined by men and boys—began to smash store windows and seize food and clothing. Confederate President Jefferson Davis himself arrived on the scene to calm the rioters. But despite Davis's appeal to Southern patriotism, the crowd refused to leave. Eventually he warned them to go home or he would order the militia to fire, and the crowd dispersed.

Curriculum Context

Shortages such as those of salt and iron show the importance of economic factors in warfare.

inadequate transportation systems, so food rotted in warehouses while civilians went hungry. The Union blockade of Southern ports began to take effect in 1862, restricting the availability of vital goods.

There was a lack of salt to preserve meat. Since the South imported most of its salt, it was never able to develop enough domestic sources to satisfy demand. Iron was also imported, so the South could not replace destroyed railroads. Leather shoes, manufactured cloth, and coffee also became increasingly scarce. Many women took out their spinning wheels and made "homespun" cloth, from which they sewed dresses. Several Southerners recorded in their diaries the pride they took in wearing homespun as a mark of their sacrifice for the war effort.

The hardships shortages created were made worse by the worthlessness of the Confederate currency. Inflation, which saw prices rise more than sevenfold, put even basic foods beyond the reach of many.

Refugees

Although families in the countryside felt the pinch of shortages and inflated prices, they were better off than those in the increasingly crowded cities. Nevertheless many rural families whose homes and farms lay in the path of invading troops decided to flee. Only a month after the war began, many northern Virginians left their homes; by 1862 the trickle had become a flood. In 1864 Ulysses S. Grant started to "squeeze the South" by

An 1864 etching by Adalbert Volck of Southern women spinning, weaving, and sewing to make clothes for Confederate soldiers.

Siege of Vicksburg

An extract from the diary of an anonymous Southern lady in Vicksburg:

"March 20th. The slow shelling of Vicksburg goes on all the time, and we have grown indifferent. It does not at present interrupt or interfere with daily avocations, but I suspect they are only getting the range of different points; and when they have them all, showers of shot will rain on us all at once. Noncombatants have been ordered to leave or prepare accordingly. Those who are to stay are having caves built. Cave-digging has become a regular business; prices range from $20 to $50. . . . Two diggers worked at ours a week and charged $30. It is well made in the hill that slopes just in the rear of the house, and well propped with thick posts, as they all are. It has a shelf, also, for holding a light or water. When we went in this evening and sat down, the earthy, suffocating feeling, as of a living tomb, was dreadful to me. I fear I shall risk death outside rather than melt in that dark furnace. The hills are so honeycombed with caves that the streets look like avenues in a cemetery."

marching his troops through the Confederacy with orders to destroy everything they found. Union General William T. Sherman's march through Georgia and the Carolinas sent more families fleeing. At least 250,000 Southerners became refugees. Most ended up in cities such as Richmond, Columbia, and Atlanta, placing increased demands on already inadequate supplies of housing, food, and public services.

Refugees
People who have been displaced from their homes, usually by warfare or natural disaster.

Often there was chaos when large communities fled before an invading army. In Columbia, South Carolina, for example, the prewar population of 8,000 had risen to 24,000 by February 1865. When Sherman's arrival became imminent, there was great confusion as officials, military personnel, and civilians all rushed to leave. Stations were jammed with people trying to board trains. Some smashed windows in their frantic attempts to escape.

When well-to-do women fled their houses, they were often forced to share quarters with poorer families who resented their presence. The refugees sometimes aggravated the situation by expressing contempt for the people with whom they sheltered.

Growing despair

As Union forces moved deeper into Confederate territory, some poorer Southerners despaired. Wives began writing to their husbands on the front line begging them to come home. Other desperate women wrote to officials about their plight, begging for help so that they might remain devoted to the cause. By the final months of the war thousands of soldiers had deserted, and officials were unable to cope with the petitions and requests that covered their desks.

There are few records of how poor Southerners reacted to the end of the war. It seems reasonable to assume, however, that many of them breathed a sigh of relief and turned their attention to their homes and farms. The planter class was much more vocal, expressing its grief and anger at Confederate defeat. As hope died, bitterness grew in its place. The legend of a Lost Cause developed during the Reconstruction era as the defeated Confederates struggled to rebuild their lives in the devastated Southern states.

Curriculum Context

You should understand the myth of the Lost Cause and its lasting influence on the South, both during and after Reconstruction.

Letter from Home

"My Dear Edward,

"I have always been proud of you, and since our connection with the Confederate Army, I have been prouder of you than ever before. I would not have you do anything wrong for the world, but before God, Edward, unless you come home, we must die. Last night I was aroused by little Eddie crying. I called and said, what is the matter, Eddie? And he said, O mamma! I am so hungry.

And Lucy, Edward, your darling Lucy, she never complains but she is getting thinner and thinner every day. And before God, Edward, unless you come home, we must die.

Your Mary"

Letter presented as evidence in support of the defendant in the court martial of a Confederate soldier, Edward Cooper, for desertion.

Home Front, Union

Civilian life in the Union was not as deeply affected by the war as in the Confederacy. The war barely touched Union soil, the larger population was not hit so hard by the draft, and the people did not go short of food as in the South.

In the autumn of 1862 a Union chaplain on leave in his native Pennsylvania was startled by the prosperity he found at home. Having grown used to war-ravaged Virginia, he wrote, "What a marvel is here! ... A nation, from internal resources alone, carrying on for over 18 months the most gigantic war of modern times, ever increasing in its magnitude, yet all the while growing richer and more prosperous!" While this glowing assessment overlooked the many wartime stresses with which Northerners had to contend, it nevertheless captured a basic truth of the conflict. The Union home front, partly from its economic strength and partly from able management, fared remarkably well compared to its Confederate counterpart.

The people of the Union

To some degree the resilience of the Union home front was to be expected, given the North's advantages in population and resources. The North's population stood at almost 22 million while the South had a population of only 9 million. The Northern population was also employed in a wider variety of occupations than in the agricultural South, and the North had a much larger manufacturing and industrial base.

Despite such advantages, if enough Northern men had not stepped forward to join the Union army, if the Northern civilian population had refused to support the war effort, or if Northern leaders had not found ways to mobilize and sustain the economy, the Union would not have been able to win the war. None of

Chaplain
A clergyman attached to part of the military.

Curriculum Context

Do you think that the North's advantages made its eventual victory in the war inevitable?

Burning a New York Orphanage

Anna Dickinson, an antislavery and women's rights campaigner, describes the burning of an African American orphanage during the New York draft riot of July 1863:

"Late in the afternoon a crowd which could have numbered not less than ten thousand, the majority of whom were ragged, frowsy, drunken women, gathered about the Orphan Asylum for Colored Children—a large and beautiful building and one of the most admirable and noble charities of the city. When it became evident ... that danger, if not destruction, was meditated to the harmless and inoffensive inmates, a flag of truce appeared, and an appeal was made on their behalf ... to every sentiment of humanity which these beings might possess—a vain appeal! Whatever human feeling had ever, if ever, filled these souls was utterly drowned and washed away in the tide of rapine and blood in which they had been steeping themselves. The few [police] officers who stood guard over the doors ... were beaten down ... while the vast crowd rushed in. ... The little ones, many of them assailed and beaten—all, orphans and caretakers, exposed to every indignity and every danger [were] driven on to the street, [and] the building was fired."

Quota
A required number of soldiers from each state.

these things happened automatically. President Lincoln's administration could call for troops, but the federal government was not large enough or strong enough to enforce that call if it was resisted. The support and cooperation of the state governments and local communities was crucial in keeping morale high and encouraging enlistment. By and large, the federal government assigned each state a quota of troops and then waited for the states to fill the quota. Local political, business, and community leaders joined forces to handle the recruitment.

Draft
A system of compulsory military service.

Initial enthusiasm to volunteer in the Union was high, and state governors asked the federal government to enlarge their quotas. The Union raised more than two million men, including more than 180,000 African Americans. Although enthusiasm waned during the war, most Union recruits were volunteers. Congress created a draft in March 1863, but it was only applied in areas that failed to meet their quotas and accounted for only 6 percent of troops.

African Americans build barricades to protect the railroad at Alexandria, Virginia, against Confederate attack in 1861. Union troops occupied the town early in the war since it lay across the Potomac River from Washington. The Union made a great effort to make the capital virtually impregnable.

The men and women who remained at home had an important role in supporting the war effort by keeping the economy buoyant. Many men remained at home to manage the farms or work in industries. They were joined by an increasing number of women in the workforce. Mostly, women served as unskilled laborers, but the war years allowed them to enter certain kinds of employment from which they had previously been barred. Until the Civil War it was almost unheard of in the United States for women to work as government clerks or as nurses, but the acute need for people to perform these functions overcame prewar prejudices.

Strikes and riots

Although the Union's economy did well overall, prices increased more steeply than wages, and laborers felt the pinch of wartime inflation. Many workers tried to negotiate for higher pay, but with little success. Some went on strike, but the strikes rarely succeeded and on a few occasions were even suppressed by the army. Once the draft was instituted in March 1863—nearly a year after the same step had been taken by the Confederacy—it became another source of discontent on the home front. To the draftees it seemed as if they were being systematically taken advantage of by wealthier Americans who could avoid the draft for a fee of $300. In several places resentment against the draft turned into violence. A number of provost officers lost their lives while attempting to enforce the draft. The

Provost officer

A member of the military police.

Curriculum Context

You may be asked to describe the different reasons for the draft riots in the North.

worst incident occurred in New York City in July 1863, when angry mobs ransacked draft offices and slaughtered dozens of free blacks, whom they blamed for the war and for conscription. At least 105 people died in the riot.

Politics and patriotism

The draft riot was an extreme manifestation of the opposition many in the Union felt to the policies of the Lincoln administration. That opposition found political expression in the Democratic Party, once the nation's largest political party and still a powerful minority. The Democrats were divided in their views on the war— most favored a war, while a significant number wanted a negotiated peace—but they were united in their opposition to emancipation, conscription, and other measures they thought violated the U.S. Constitution and the philosophy of limited government. They created the Society for the Diffusion of Political Knowledge, an organization to publish pamphlets critical of Lincoln's administration. The Republicans responded with two organizations of their own, the Loyal Publication Society and the Union League, which printed nearly 5 million pro-administration pamphlets.

Curriculum Context

It is important to be aware of wider criticism within the North of Lincoln's administration, particularly of its curbing of civil liberties.

Benevolent societies

An important contribution to the war effort was made by voluntary organizations. Soldiers' Aid Associations raised funds, collected supplies, and donated facilities. The U.S. Sanitary Commission, created in 1861, was formed in response to concern about the health and medical care of Union soldiers. It employed paid agents to inspect Northern camps and assigned doctors and ambulances to accompany the armies on active campaign. Huge numbers of people in the Union supported it—and similar organizations—with both money and volunteer assistance. Sanitary fairs in several large Northern cities raised millions of dollars to help the Union war effort.

Life in the border states

In the Union border states civilian life was deeply affected by the war. Kentucky tried to remain neutral but suffered invasion by troops from both sides. Families were split by their loyalty to either side perhaps more than in any other state. In Maryland the Union government came down hard on the supporters of secession. Parts of the state were under occupation, state elections were manipulated, and civilians were imprisoned without trial. The border state of Missouri suffered 1,162 battles and skirmishes (a total exceeded only in Virginia and Tennessee), as pro-Union and pro-Confederate guerrilla bands terrorized civilians.

War and society

The impact of war on civilian life lasted beyond 1865. The increased power of the federal government continued into the Reconstruction Period (1865–1877). Women remained in the workforce. Their involvement in war-related volunteer efforts may have enhanced their status in society but did not secure them the vote until 50 years later. The service of African Americans in the Union army altered their place in Northern society, although equality remained far in the future.

Civilian Fund Raising

Many Northern cities held sanitary fairs to raise funds to buy medical supplies for wounded soldiers, and other types of relief. The first such event was held in Chicago on October 27, 1863. The organizers—Mary Livermore and Jane Hoge of the U.S. Sanitary Commission—encouraged people to donate items of interest that they could sell to raise funds. The Chicago fair ran for two weeks and drew 5,000 visitors. The entrance price was 75 cents, and the items on sale included artwork, musical instruments, toys, and clothes. President Lincoln donated the original draft of the Emancipation Proclamation, which was the fair's main attraction and sold at auction for $3,000. The Chicago fair raised $100,000, and following its success, other major cities held fairs. The largest sanitary fair was held in New York in April 1864. Visitors could buy trinkets made by Confederate prisoners of war or even bid for a tame bear or a shipload of coal.

Houses and Furniture

The style of houses and furnishings popular during the Civil War era was known as "Victorian" for Queen Victoria, who ruled Great Britain between 1837 and 1901. The style was very ornate, and dark furniture and rich colors were fashionable.

In the 1860s fashionable houses were large, gabled dwellings with porches and "gingerbread" trim painted in shades of yellow, red, and brown. Inside, rooms shone with rich colors—deep carmine, gilt, and sky blue—and were filled with a clutter of parlor suites, writing bureaus, coatracks, tables, and chairs. During the Civil War intricate and rich interiors were popular.

Victorian values

The term "Victorian" refers to the culture of English-speaking peoples on both sides of the Atlantic Ocean in the 19th century. Britain and the United States were rapidly industrializing, which led to more Americans becoming part of the middle class. Along with owners of businesses, doctors, lawyers, teachers, and ministers, this group expanded to include salaried employees who worked as managers, technicians, clerks, and engineers. These people now worked in towns and cities. Long working hours earned their families a modest status and enough money to live in some style and comfort. They wanted houses and furnishings to match their new rank.

A prosperous city dweller in the North might build a two-story masonry house. A less well-off clerk in the city might move his family to the new suburbs away from the noise, dirt, and danger of the city, where he could build a house. A poor family in the city could only afford to rent a small apartment in a tenement building shared with other lodgers. In rural areas of the North a family lived in farmhouses, either new or old.

Curriculum Context

Do you think that the emergence of a strong middle class was an inevitable consequence of a more industrial and urban society?

In the Southern states a wealthy merchant in New Orleans might live in a fashionable two-story brick dwelling. In other commercial centers, like Savannah, Charleston, and Richmond, there were many stylish and up-to-date houses. Rural areas had a quite different architecture. A nonslaveholding farmer's home was a simple wooden frame house, which had little in common with the slave huts or the elegant plantation home of a wealthy landowner nearby.

In all but the most expensive houses people used building materials that were close by and plentiful. In forested areas people built wooden frame houses and log cabins. In the Southwest, where the dry climate meant there was little vegetation, people built houses of adobe bricks.

Architectural styles

Very wealthy people built homes in a specific style: popular styles were Gothic Revival—inspired by European medieval architecture with features such as pointed arches and battlements—and the Italianate style, which was influenced by Italian country villas. A distinctive feature was the use of brackets, or L-shaped pieces of carved wood up under the eaves. Italianate houses had low-pitched or flat roofs; and were painted in blues, greens, and yellows.

Adobe

A building material made out of mud, often mixed with straw and dried in the sun.

An 1873 illustration of a kitchen in Boston, Massachusetts. In the center is the kitchen range, which was found in most new homes of the time, and was used for cooking as well as heating water.

The Hatrack

Ellen Bowie Holland in her memoir of her girlhood in North Texas, remembers one piece of furniture:

"A hatrack was a very articulate piece of furniture. From the conglomeration hanging on it, at a glance, you could tell if Uncle Harry, Cousin Frank, or the Misses McGruders were being entertained—and it was exciting to see a strange flowered hat, a city derby, or a feather boa. Our hatrack was the biggest, ugliest piece of furniture made since they divided all Gaul into three parts. But we didn't know it. It was simply accepted as a necessity. It was of oak and around a mirror bristled six fancy double brass prongs. The lower part was an armed seat and the top of the seat was hinged like a chest. It opened and when we came home we dumped our extra fribbles into it. Whenever anything was lost someone would say, 'Have you looked in the hatrack?'"

Symmetrical

A design in which each half is a reflection or copy of the other.

The fine homes of the prewar South continued the earlier Greek Revival style, inspired by ancient Greece. The houses had a symmetrical floor plan with a wide central hall that let air circulate freely during the warmer months. They were white, with tall windows that reached the floor. The front often resembled a Greek temple's entrance with tall pillars. A decade after the Civil War, the fashionable architectural styles of the Victorian era appeared in the South.

House designs

Much American architecture was "vernacular," which means commonplace. In 19th-century America the profession of architecture was just starting. A few architects did publish plan books, which included line drawings of exteriors and floor plans. Builders copied these designs for wealthy clients. Soon afterward Americans had opportunities to buy plans for their homes from magazines and mail-order catalogues.

Curriculum Context

The growth of mail-order retailing had an interesting influence on the changing life on the Western frontier.

Inside the home

The outside appearance of a house was a good indication of a family's status and wealth. The interior of a house was expected to provide a different space from the materialistic world of work. The home was to serve as a place of spiritual renewal in which family members would want to gather. The interior decoration therefore took on a special meaning. Special magazines and books advised on selecting colors, furniture, lighting, and wallpapers.

In the Victorian era men presided over the house, while women were responsible for creating interior spaces that provided a comfortable living space and displayed how cultured the family was. They accomplished this by decorating the home with handiwork such as embroidery or painted china. The furniture may have been handed down through the family, bought from local cabinetmakers, or imported from manufacturers in the big cities. New furniture often took inspiration from old historical styles, such as Gothic, Elizabethan, Rococo, and Louis XVI.

Heating and plumbing
Builders took the climate into consideration when building houses, since there was no air-conditioning or central heating. Electricity came much later in the century. Candles or kerosene lamps lit the rooms. A few houses had gas lighting, especially in cities. Very few homes had running water, this meant all water had to be drawn by hand, and chamberpots and outhouses were used instead of flush toilets.

Polite behavior
Before the Victorian period rooms usually served several purposes. Now rooms became specialized. A hall, formal parlor, family parlor, dining room, library, bedroom—all served specific functions and required certain activities and behavior. Knowing how to behave appropriately in these settings, following the social rules correctly, defined a person's place in society and showed whether or not he or she was a refined person. In a rapidly changing society these complex rules of behavior helped establish the social order.

Kerosene
A flammable oil produced by distilling petroleum.

Outhouse
An outside bathroom that is not attached to a house.

Curriculum Context

Why might people have been so concerned about maintaining social order during a time of war?

Immigrants

A surge in immigration in the decades before the Civil War meant that by 1860 the ethnic composition of the United States was rapidly changing. More than 500,000 foreign-born soldiers fought in the war, overwhelmingly for the Union.

Curriculum Context

You might be asked to describe the impact of immigration on the size of cities in the United States.

A huge majority of the immigrant populations settled in the free-labor states of the North rather than the South, which contributed to the feeling the two were growing further apart. Immigration played a major part in the political turmoil and disintegration that led to a party realignment along sectional lines in the late 1850s, and then to secession and war.

Immigration was not a large part of life during the first 50 years of American independence. Even in the 1820s, when immigrant numbers began to grow, there were fewer than 130,000 new arrivals (representing just 1 in 100 out of a population of 13 million in 1830). Between 1830 and 1840, there was a quadrupling of immigrants. As had been the case from the Republic's earliest days, the great majority were Protestants, mainly from Britain; and while many were farmers, many others were skilled or white-collar workers.

Curriculum Context

The causes of the wave of immigration from northern Europe are studied in many curricula.

Dramatic change

During the 1840s and 1850s a dramatic change in immigration took place. Repeated potato crop failures in Ireland and political and economic upheaval in Germany created a huge influx of immigration to the United States. Just under 1.5 million arrived in the 1840s and 2.8 million in the 1850s. Since the population was 31 million in 1860, that meant nearly 1 in every 10 Americans had arrived in the previous decade. More than 60 percent of these new immigrants were Roman Catholics from Ireland and Germany, and a great many of the Irish were poor, unskilled laborers.

Overwhelmingly this influx was concentrated in the large cities of the Northeast, in New York, Boston, and Philadelphia, where squalid, overcrowded tenements became a feature of urban life. By 1860, 39 percent of the foreign-born population of the United States was Irish and 31 percent German.

Immigration on this scale and of this type did not go unchallenged. There were sporadic anti-Catholic riots in the big cities, and "nativist" political parties emerged that attempted to slow down the pace at which immigrants could achieve full citizenship rights. The nativist political movement helped contribute to the breakdown of the existing two-party system that preceded the Civil War. In the end it was the antislavery Republican Party that emerged from the ruins of the Whig Party in the 1850s, but in the early years of the decade a powerful new nativist party known as the Know-Nothings was attracting considerable political support among native-born Americans.

Nativist

Someone who supports policies favoring "native" inhabitants over immigrants; "native" Americans did not include indigenous peoples.

The Know-Nothings

The nativist Know-Nothings were a powerful political force in the decade leading up to the Civil War. Their origins lay in a number of secret fraternal orders whose membership was restricted to native-born Protestants. From 1852 these organizations were welded together into a national force with perhaps as many as a million members. The members pledged to vote only for native-born Protestants and to fend off any questions from outsiders by responding, "I know nothing." This led to them being dubbed "Know-Nothings," and the name stuck.

Because of their secrecy and commitment, the Know-Nothings were a powerful political influence, and they helped polarize many of the burning issues of the day, including slavery. The Democratic Party was seen as the immigrant's friend, and Irish Catholics in particular overwhelmingly supported it. The Democratic Party was also seen as slavery's friend, however. Know-Nothings were thus inclined to link slavery with Catholicism as something that was fundamentally foreign to the American way of life. By 1860, however, the Know-Nothings had largely faded from the scene as a political force since the new Republican Party seemed to have a more secure grip on the impending crisis over the slavery issue.

Wartime immigration

During the first two years of the war immigration fell sharply, but picked up again in 1863 because of labor shortages. Many immigrants jumped at the generous bounties offered to join the Union army: of the two million white men who fought in Union colors, about one in four was foreign-born. This gave rise to the Southern charge that the Union was fighting the war with "foreign hirelings." Lincoln made an effort to court immigrants in the 1860 election and rewarded their leaders with army appointments. Despite suffering hostility from native-born Americans in the 1850s, various nationalities raised companies, including Irish, Scandinavian, French, Italian, and German units. Several units, such as the Irish Brigade, achieved fame for their bravery. The immigrant volunteers often brought valuable military experience from Europe.

Draft riots

In July 1863 riots broke out in New York City in protest at the Conscription Act. The act was seen as unfair because a man could avoid military service for a fee of $300 or by hiring a substitute. Irish immigrants were prominent in looting and violence that lasted for four days and nights. By the time it petered out on July 17, the city was shattered, and more than 100 people had been killed.

Curriculum Context

What reasons might have encouraged immigrants to fight for the Union?

Curriculum Context

Students are expected to understand that immigration was one of many causes of the draft riots in the North.

An 1866 engraving of the first immigrant-processing center in the United States, set up in 1855 on Castle Garden, an island off Manhattan, New York.

Industry

In 1860 the United States was poised to become a great industrial power, but its industry was concentrated in the Northern states. The small industrial base in the South hampered the efforts of the Confederacy to supply its fighting forces during the war.

Two key divisions between the North and South existed on the eve of war: Southern slavery and the rapid Northern industrialization. The South's industrial backwardness was one of the Confederacy's gravest handicaps and plagued its war effort throughout.

Before the war, Southern economic subordination to the North was a hotly debated issue. It irritated proud Southerners to see their region slipping behind the free states, but it also reinforced their belief the South was unique—a stable farming community that protected an attractive way of life for whites. They also argued that industrial workers in the North were no better off than slaves. The poverty and overcrowding in Northern cities and the inhumanity of long working hours in airless factories for a pittance was proof. Envy of Northern prosperity was mixed with contempt for the methods that made progress possible.

The widening gulf

The industrial gulf between the two regions widened in the two decades before the war. In 1840 there were nearly as many miles of railroad in the slave states as free states. By 1860, in relation to its population and size, the North was about twice as well served by rail as the South. Four-fifths of the nation's factories were in the free states, and accounted for nearly 90 percent of total manufacturing. Cotton textile manufacture in the South, where the bulk of the world's raw cotton was grown, represented only 10 percent of the American total in 1860. The figure for the manufacture of boots

Curriculum Context

Students may be expected to be able to summarize the differences between the North and the South at the start of the war.

Curriculum Context

Why might the nation's industry be concentrated in the Northern states?

and shoes was the same. Northern states made 93 percent of the nation's pig iron (crude iron as it comes out of the blast furnace) and 97 percent of its firearms.

Complacency about the superiority of the Southern way of life was difficult to sustain in the face of such evidence. In a series of annual conventions that took place before the start of war, progressive Southerners debated ways to shake the region out of its commercial sleepiness. There were calls to set up a shipbuilding industry so the South could trade directly with Europe. There was also agitation to build a railroad west to the Pacific Coast. Plans were put forward to build factories to provide the economic strength and diversity to resist the mounting political pressure from the free states.

Progressives

People who believe that economic development will help introduce beneficial social change.

Urgent need for industry

While industrial activity in the Southern states improved during the 1850s, the war exposed its limitations. When the Union naval blockade began to strangle Southern trade, the Confederacy realized the urgent need to expand its industry at home. In a break with prewar tradition, government departments allocated resources to build factories. Gunpowder mills and ordnance factories were built in cities such as Atlanta and Richmond. The Tredegar Works honored its pledge to produce enough iron to meet almost all the Confederacy's military and transportation needs. Despite huge difficulties, Confederate industry did keep the army supplied with guns and ammunition to the end. The industrial advances were not permanent, as Union armies destroyed many new industries.

Curriculum Context

Is it the job of government to build factories? Shouldn't that be left to the free market?

Industry in the Union flourishes

The Union's initial industrial superiority was magnified during the war partly in response to the increase in demand for equipment and supplies, but also because of changes in the labor market. The shortage of labor led to rapid improvements in mechanization. In the

Ribbons of Steel

Railroads were extremely important during the Civil War for both civilian and military purposes. They continued their prewar activities of transporting people and goods while also serving to move large numbers of troops and supplies over great distances. At the outset of war the Confederacy closed the Mississippi River to Union traffic, but the North was able to rely instead on its existing east–west rail systems, which included the Baltimore & Ohio, the Erie, and the Pennsylvania. Railroad building slowed down in the North in the first years of the war, but the existing system was well maintained and then expanded by the capture of railroads in the Confederacy. The Confederacy, on the other hand, lacked the resources to expand or even to maintain its existing railroad network, which by 1865 lay virtually in ruins. Meanwhile, the Union had sufficient manpower and resources to start work on the first transcontinental railroad in 1863 and laid 20 miles (32km) of track eastward from Sacramento, California.

garment industry the sewing machine vastly increased the production of military uniforms and other clothing. Many more women were employed in industry and agriculture. With nearly a million Northern farmers under arms, farm productivity rose rapidly in the Union due to revolutionary new reapers and harvesters and the enthusiasm of the farming women.

The economic productivity of the Union was startling. In 1864 iron production was nearly a third higher than it had ever been for the whole country and coal production increased similarly. Merchant ship-building increased; the Union navy grew to nearly 700 ships—making it the largest in the world. An armaments industry that in 1861 could not begin to equip the Union armies was more than able to do so by 1865, despite the huge growth in army numbers. Canal and railroad traffic soared as the internal market boomed. The industrial triumph of the Union heralded the success of postwar American industry, which overtook the industry of Great Britain and Germany within a generation of the Civil War.

Curriculum Context

Farm machinery was a good example of technological innovation that was partly inspired by the demands of the war.

Merchant ship

A vessel that is used to transport trade goods and passengers, as opposed to a warship.

Invention and Technology

The Civil War saw major advances in technology. Generals used the electric telegraph to coordinate the movements of vast armies, while both sides faced highly destructive new weapons such as concealed mines and the machine gun.

The great advances in technology made during the war were partly due to the 19th-century enthusiasm for scientific innovation and partly to the belief that new technology would help both sides fight the war more efficiently. The war sparked a race among inventors to develop rapid-fire small arms such as breechloading rifles and machine guns. Older types of weapons were used in innovative ways—heavy artillery was mounted on railroad cars, giving it a new flexibility. The naval war saw the deployment of sea mines (then called torpedoes) and submarines—both developed by the Confederacy during the war to defend its coastline against the Union navy.

The war exploited the potential of some prewar inventions. The sewing machine, invented in 1846, allowed Union factories to clothe vast armies, and the electric telegraph revolutionized communications.

The 13-inch (33-cm) Union mortar known as the "Dictator" mounted on a railroad car in October 1864 during the Siege of Petersburg, Virginia. Giant mortars were traditionally used in coastal forts. The Union used railroads to transform them into portable guns.

The telegraph, introduced in the 1840s, had spread across the country by 1861. During the war telegraph lines were laid along the routes of the armies, keeping the war departments in Washington, D.C., and Richmond informed. It allowed Civil War generals to employ strategies on a scale not seen before in war. In May 1864 General-in-chief of the Union army, Ulysses S. Grant, gave daily orders to his armies in Virginia, Georgia, and West Virginia, thus coordinating the operations of more than half a million soldiers.

Infernal machines

The Civil War spurred the development of many of the weapons that dominated 20th century warfare. The Confederacy, outnumbered by Union forces and desperate to defend territory, developed land mines (known as torpedoes). They were first used by General Gabriel J. Rains to halt the Union army's advance during the Peninsular Campaign in 1862. The rank-and-file on both sides dubbed these concealed mines "infernal machines." But they proved their worth, and the Confederacy allocated more money for their development. By 1864 Rains had been given a budget of $350,000 by the Confederate Congress to lay land mines to defend Richmond. That year he supervised the laying of over 1,200 mines around the city.

Infernal
Related to hell.

Sea mines

The Confederates also developed several types of sea mine to sink Union navy ships. The Russian navy had used sea mines in a limited way during the Crimean War (1853–1856), but in the Civil War they proved their destructive potential. A Civil War sea mine was a watertight cylinder made from tin or sheet-iron and packed with gunpowder. It had an air-filled chamber to give it buoyancy. Sea mines floated just below the water surface and were anchored to the seabed by cable. They could be detonated by an enemy vessel pulling on a trigger wire attached to a float. The most

A Union signal telegraph machine and operator, sketched by war artist Alfred Waud at Fredericksburg in 1862.

sophisticated device used was the electric detonator, which was triggered by wire from shore. It was first used on the Yazoo River, Mississippi, in 1862 to sink the USS *Cairo*. No Civil War sea mine was self-propelled, although there were experiments with such weapons. Instead, mines were attached to vessels by a spar (long wooden pole). The spar was then rammed into an enemy ship. These "spar torpedoes" were fitted to small, fast vessels, converting the boats into destructive warships. By the end of the war Confederate mines had sunk 29 Union vessels and damaged 14, which made the mine the most effective weapon used by the Confederates against the Union navy.

Warships

The naval war saw the deployment of two of the most innovative types of warship ever built: submarines and ironclads. The Confederate submarine CSS *Hunley* was the first submarine to sink an enemy vessel in wartime when it rammed the USS *Housatonic* with a spar torpedo on February 17, 1864, in Charleston harbor. The *Hunley* and its eight-man crew sank soon after the attack. The cause of the sinking remains a mystery. The USS *Monitor* was a steam-propelled and iron-plated warship, known as an ironclad. It has been called the first modern warship. The *Monitor*'s most innovative feature was its rotating iron gun turret. *Monitor*'s battle with the Confederate ironclad CSS *Virginia* in Hampton Roads, Virginia, on March 9, 1862, led the Union navy to commission many ironclad vessels of the same design.

New firearms

One of the major technological advances for Civil War soldiers was the breechloading repeating rifle, because it was quick to load and allowed the user to fire several

Breechloading
A rifle that is loaded through a chamber in the barrel, not from the end of the barrel.

shots before reloading. The Henry, a more advanced rifle, was only introduced in the last year of the war. Its 15-shot magazine could be emptied in just 11 seconds. During the war there was a race to invent the first practical machine gun to provide rapid, continuous fire.

The Gatling gun

The Gatling, invented by Richard Gatling in 1862, was a six-barreled gun that used a rotating mechanism to load, fire, and eject ammunition at a (then) phenomenal rate of 200 rounds per minute. The gun had several drawbacks. It was too big and heavy to be maneuverable in rough country and it used gunpowder, which produced dense clouds of smoke that obscured the target. During the Civil War, only 12 Gatling guns were used by the Union army. Gatling himself sincerely believed his invention would bring an end to war because the carnage his new weapon could inflict would make any future war unthinkable.

Curriculum Context

Should Gatling be condemned for creating an instrument of death, whatever his beliefs about its effects?

The Invention of the Telegraph

The electric telegraph revolutionized communications around the world in the mid-19th century. In 1825 the British inventor William Sturgeon (1783–1850) exhibited an electromagnet—a bar of iron surrounded by coils of copper wire that could be turned into a magnet by passing an electric current through the wire. The electric signal could be switched on and off, causing the magnet to either press a lever or move a marker.

In the United States in the 1830s Samuel F.B. Morse (1791–1872) used the signal to create a communication system. It consisted of an operator key and a receiver. When the key was pressed, it completed an electric circuit and sent a signal to the receiver, which turned on the magnet. This then moved a mechanism that made an indentation on a paper roll or, later in the 1850s, made a sound that the operator could hear. The Morse Code used combinations of short and long signals (dots and dashes) that were decoded by the operator at the receiving end.

In 1844 the first stretch of telegraph line was laid on wooden poles along 35 miles (56km) of railroad track between Washington, D.C., and Baltimore, Maryland. The system began operation on May 24, 1844, with the message: "What hath God wrought."

Literature

The Civil War took place during the 19th-century flowering of American literature known as the American Renaissance. The cataclysmic effect of the war resulted in a huge amount of literature of varying quality being produced both during and after the conflict.

Curriculum Context

You'll need to know about *Uncle Tom's Cabin* to be able to describe fully the pressures in the North for the abolition of slavery.

One book closely associated with the Civil War, which is said to have been a cause of the conflict, was published a decade before the first shot was fired. *Uncle Tom's Cabin*, Harriet Beecher Stowe's bestselling novel of 1852, was an indictment of the fugitive-slave laws. The novel brought the horrors of slavery to a wider audience, especially in the North, where many people had little or no experience of slavery. It helped strengthen support for the abolitionist movement, deepening the divisions between North and South.

Wartime literature

Some of the earliest literary responses to the war were patriotic songs. The Union had "The Battle-Hymn of the Republic," while the best-known Confederate songs included "Maryland, My Maryland" and "The Bonnie Blue Flag." The Quaker poet John Greenleaf Whittier wrote the well-loved pro-Union poem "Barbara Frietchie" in 1863. He based his poem on an incident in which an old woman waved her Union flag as General "Stonewall" Jackson and his Confederates rode through Frederick, Maryland. Barbara Frietchie was a real person, but almost certainly not involved in any such incident.

Curriculum Context

Students may be expected to understand how individuals such as Whitman fit with common themes in American art and literature.

Poetry in the 1860s

One of the most original poetic voices of the period, and of the 19th century, was Walt Whitman. He produced two collections of poems during the war and made revisions and additions to his most famous work, *Leaves of Grass*, first published in 1855.

The other leading poet of the Civil War was Emily Dickinson. She wrote some 800 poems but only seven of her poems were published in her lifetime, and none at all under her own name. After the war, there was a glut of poetry anthologies. Among the most important collections of poetry were H.H. Brownell's *War Lyrics* (1866), a book of verse by Union poets, and *War Poetry of the South* (1866), an anthology of Confederate poems.

Curriculum Context

It might be useful to compare the views of the Northern and Southern poets. Do they have any common themes?

Merely Not Dying

Most of the writers who emerged in the aftermath of the Civil War were from the North, since the South was shattered culturally as well as economically. "Perhaps as you know," Southern poet Sidney Lanier wrote to a friend, "that, with us of the younger generation in the

Emily Dickinson

Emily Elizabeth Dickinson was one of the foremost American poets of the 19th century. She was born in Amherst, Massachusetts, on December 10, 1830. After graduating from Amherst Academy in 1847, she attended nearby Mount Holyoke Female Seminary for one year. Despite considerable pressure to become a Christian, she refused. Although many of her poems deal with God, she remained a skeptic for the rest of her life.

Dickinson began to write poetry in the 1850s. Her poems were unconventional and deceptively simple lyrics that were usually concerned with death, eternity, and the inner life. The Civil War years saw her greatest literary output: Between 1862 and 1866 she wrote more than a third of her poems. In April 1862 she wrote to the critic Thomas Wentworth Higginson asking for his opinion on her poems. Although he was impressed by their originality in form and content—irregular rhythms adapted from the meters of hymns, eccentric phrasing and syntax, and emotional intensity and candor—he advised her against publication.

By the late 1860s Dickinson had become a recluse, dressing always in white. During her final decades she never left her house and garden. Although she chose to publish only a handful of poems in her lifetime, she never doubted that her poetry would be well received. After she died in 1886, her sister decided to have her poems published. The first collection, *Poems by Emily Dickinson*, appeared in 1890. Dickinson's reputation grew gradually, and she is now regarded as one of the greatest of all poets.

Walt Whitman's Civil War

Late in 1862 the poet Walt Whitman went to the battlefront in Virginia to find his brother George, who was wounded at Fredericksburg while serving in the Union army. After spending some time in camp, Whitman returned to Washington, D.C., where he worked in various government departments. He served as a volunteer nurse to soldiers of both sides who lay sick and dying in unhygienic military hospitals. He wrote letters home for them and supplied invalids with food and other necessities, which he paid for out of his own small salary.

Whitman's wartime experiences directly inspired two volumes of poetry: *Drum-Taps* (1865) and *Sequel to Drum-Taps* (1865–1866). The latter contains two of his most famous works— "When Lilacs Last in the Dooryard Bloom'd" and "O Captain! My Captain!" Both poems express the sadness that Walt Whitman felt on the assassination of President Lincoln shortly after the end of the war in 1865. A prose volume, *Specimen Days* (1882), was an autobiographical account of Whitman's work as a wartime nurse.

Curriculum Context

Students studying Reconstruction should be aware of the widespread nostalgia for the prewar South and be able to judge its relation to reality.

South since the War, pretty much the whole of life has been merely not dying." This feeling of hopelessness is also reflected in the poetry of Henry Timrod and Paul Hamilton Hayne, who both looked back nostalgically to the prewar period. Lanier was the most innovative postwar Southern poet. A talented musician, he saw verse as a "phenomenon of sound" and in *The Science of English Verse* (1880) made an analysis of poetics in terms of musical notation, anticipating many poets of the 20th century.

Memories of the war

Immediately after the war most people wanted to put the horrors of the conflict behind them. However, from the 1870s there was a flood of autobiographies and reminiscences written by men from both sides, from generals to ordinary soldiers. The most celebrated of the autobiographies was by Ulysses S. Grant, the Union general and president. He wrote his *Personal Memoirs* while dying of throat cancer and barely completed them before his death in 1885. His style was straightforward, restrained, and objective and avoided

Curriculum Context

An understanding of Grant's wartime experiences and his philosophy is very helpful for anyone studying his presidency.

apporting blame. It became a classic and in a short time after his death earned Grant's family $450,000.

In the 1880s *Century* magazine published a series of illustrated articles about the war by those who took part. In 1888 they were collected in a four-volume set called *Battles and Leaders of the Civil War*, which is still a valuable eyewitness account of the war. The novelist Louisa May Alcott (1832–1888) found fame with the publication of *Hospital Sketches* (1863), the letters she wrote as a Civil War nurse in Washington, D.C. Her hugely popular semiautobiographical novel *Little Women* (1868) follows four sisters during the Civil War.

There was a great interest in stories that took place in a particular part of the country and gave descriptions of the landscape, local customs, and dialects of a certain place. Thomas Nelson Page wrote stories of plantation life in Virginia, narrated in black dialect. They depicted

Dialect
A regional variety of a language, which is usually distinguished by its sounds, grammar, and unique words.

Whitman's Poetry

Extract from Walt Whitman's poem about the assassination of Abraham Lincoln, "When Lilacs Last in the Dooryard Bloom'd"

Nor for you, for one alone,
Blossoms and branches green to coffins all I bring,
For fresh as the morning, thus would I chant a song for you
O sane and sacred death.
All over bouquets of roses,
O death, I cover you over with roses and early lilies,
But mostly and now the lilac that blooms the first,
Copious I break, I break the sprigs from the bushes,
With loaded arms I come, pouring for you,
For you and the coffins all of you O death.

A poster advertising Harriet Beecher Stowe's Uncle Tom's Cabin. The novel was an instant success and sold 300,000 copies in its first year. It was quickly adapted into a play that was also very popular.

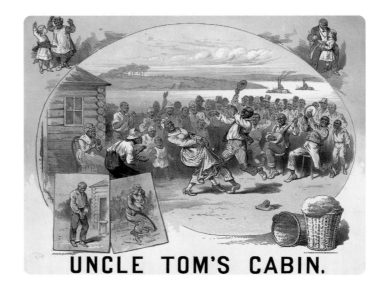

UNCLE TOM'S CABIN.

the South, before and after the Civil War, as an ordered and happy society. Similarly, *Uncle Remus: His Songs and His Sayings* (1881), by Joel Chandler Harris, evoked a romanticized past swept away by Reconstruction. Such novels were popular among nostalgic Southerners and Northerners who were fascinated by a world they had never known. The influence of this style of writing, which evokes a strong sense of place, is clearly seen in the works of Mark Twain, such as *The Adventures of Huckleberry Finn* (1884). Twain had briefly joined a Confederate militia, but his main contribution to the Civil War was as publisher of Grant's memoirs.

Curriculum Context

Crane was born after the Civil War ended; on what grounds might such a writer be praised for his "realistic" battle scenes? Can fictional works help our understanding of the conflict as a whole?

Later works

The first major work of fiction about the Civil War by an author born after the end of the conflict was *The Red Badge of Courage* (1895), by Stephen Crane. The novel was praised for its realism and vivid depictions of battle scenes. The most celebrated novel about the Civil War is *Gone with the Wind* (1936), by Margaret Mitchell. This 1,000-page Pulitzer Prize-winning romance about the destruction of the Old South became the bestselling novel in U.S. history and the basis for a film in 1939 that is among the most famous movies ever made.

Money and Banking

The Civil War severely strained the economic systems of both the Union and the Confederacy. It was clear that the side that could raise the largest amount of money would have the greater chance of winning on the battlefield.

In early 1861 American finance was largely in the hands of private banks. They issued paper money that could be exchanged for gold or silver ("specie"). The money supply was determined mainly by how much specie was in circulation at any given time. Taxes were low. The federal government received most of its income from import taxes (tariffs) and the sale of public lands.

It quickly became clear the war would force changes in this way of thinking. In the summer of 1861 Union Treasury Secretary Salmon P. Chase negotiated a loan of $150 million in specie from banks. The government was to repay the loans by selling $250 million of bonds. Bonds were government certificates guaranteeing the bearer it would pay back the initial sum with interest.

Legal Tender Act

Initially, the war went badly for the Union. Bond sales and tax collections were less than expected, and people hoarded specie. Finally, on December 30 the government decided bank notes no longer had to be backed by the same amount in gold reserves. Knowing that state banks were now free to print an unlimited amount of money, which could cause uncontrolled inflation, Congress decided to preempt the state banks: In February 1862 Congress passed the Legal Tender Act, allowing the treasury to issue $150 million worth of paper money not backed by specie. The bills became known as "greenbacks" because they were printed with green ink. By the end of the war the government had issued $450 million in greenbacks.

Union taxes and bonds

New taxes were added throughout the war, including the first income tax. But the sale of bonds proved more important to the Union government and paid for about two-thirds of the war's cost. In 1862 Congress approved the sale of $500 million of bonds at 6 percent interest.

National Banking Act

In December 1861 Chase asked Congress to create a system of national banks to issue a standardized currency. His proposal met with opposition but finally, in February 1863, Congress passed the National Banking Act. Banks could obtain a federal charter (license) by investing at least one-third of their capital in government bonds. They could then issue money up to 90 percent of the value of the bonds. In the short run the main effect of the act was to stimulate demand for war bonds; the new national bank currency did not replace greenbacks or state bank notes. In the long run, however, the act shifted important financial functions to the federal government and away from the states, and that had far-reaching effects.

Confederate failure

While the Confederacy used the same basic tools as the Union—bonds, taxes, and paper money—it did so with much poorer planning and never matched the Union's financial acumen. More important, the Confederate economy lacked the underlying strength to maintain public confidence, a key to making currency and bonds hold their value. Finally, due to its emphasis on states' rights the Confederate government lacked the authority to do many of the things that the Union did. There was no Confederate equivalent of the National Banking Act. By the end of the war Confederate money had experienced an inflation rate of 9,000 percent, suggesting that the South's declining fortunes on the battlefield and the declining value of its currency were closely linked.

Curriculum Context

Students may be asked for examples of how the federal government grew stronger as a result of the Civil War at the expense of state governments.

Curriculum Context

Some curricula encourage students to study the connection between military success on the battlefield and economic and technological success away from the fighting.

Plantation Life

The planter class in the South consisted of white families who owned 20 slaves or more to work their fields, do their laundry, cook, and keep their houses. For the planters it was a life of comfort; for the slaves, one of toil and constraint.

In 1860 a quarter of Southern white families owned slaves. By law they could buy African American slaves to work for them without pay. As with all property, the number of slaves a white family owned reflected the family's wealth and social class. About 960,000 of all slave owners in the South (12 percent of the white population of 8 million) belonged to the planter class of landowners who had 20 or more slaves. At the very top of the social pyramid were about 2,500 masters who owned more than 100 slaves.

Although three-quarters of whites in the South could not afford to own slaves, most still supported the system. They were linked to the planter class by family and economic ties, they aspired to own slaves, and even poor and illiterate whites felt they were members of the ruling classes as a result of their race.

Curriculum Context

Why do you think that Southerners without slaves felt that slavery was a desirable system?

Hard labor

Owning slaves was a badge of status, but crucially it also provided a source of labor. The Southern planter was a businessman who usually grew just one crop for profit. Most slaves worked as field hands and endured long working hours from sunup to sundown. Their work varied by region and crop. Most slaves worked on cotton plantations. In the Chesapeake area (Virginia and Maryland) the chief crop was tobacco. Tobacco farms were smaller and did not produce large profits, so masters and slaves often worked side by side. Most tobacco planters looked after their slaves relatively well because they could not easily afford to replace them.

This plantation house built in Charleston, South Carolina, was typical of the luxurious homes of the planter class in the South.

The richest slave owners were rice growers in coastal areas of Georgia and South Carolina. The hot and humid climate made these plantations a breeding ground for diseases. Rice planters and their families could afford to leave their farms to be supervised by a paid white overseer during the hot summer months.

Household slaves

On large plantations there was a group of household slaves who lived close to the planter family. They usually had better living conditions than field hands, and were better fed since they had access to leftovers from the family table. But they had little privacy since they lived in their owner's house. The harsh reality was that slave women were very vulnerable to the advances of masters. They also suffered at the hand of plantation mistresses who could punish female slaves with beatings or by giving them increased workloads.

Resisting oppression

Although slaves were property with no rights in the eyes of the law, they found ways of showing their resistance. Escape was practically impossible and revolts could be suicidal, so slaves resisted in other ways. Feigning sickness or working slowly were common ploys. Others committed acts of sabotage by breaking tools or fences.

Because slave marriages were not legally recognized, and the master had the power to separate families at will, slaves used the "extended kin" of friends to provide support and comfort should a family be split apart. There was no formal education for slaves and it was illegal for whites to teach slaves to read and write. Religion, music, and folk stories were crucial in keeping alive a vibrant African American culture.

Curriculum Context

Some curricula expect students to be aware of the various ways in which slaves preserved elements of their African heritage.

Southern violence

Slavery was built on violence. Slave children were often beaten by their white slave owners and their parents, who had to teach them to obey in order to survive in such a harsh world. Slave children were often left on their own because their mothers were rarely allowed free time to spend with their children. Although black and white children often played together, white children grew up to be the owners of their one-time playmates. A Virginia planter recalled how as a child he cried when he saw slave children beaten. But by the time he reached manhood, he could not only witness a whipping but inflicted the lashes himself without pity.

Efficiency and Profit

The vast majority of slaves worked on cotton plantations in gangs under the supervision of an overseer, who was generally a white man. Next in line was the slave driver, who was usually drawn from among the slave population. Most slaves worked six days a week. At nightfall during the harvest season the amount of cotton each slave had picked would be weighed. Those who had not picked as much as usual might be subjected to harsh physical punishment, while any slave who had picked more would be expected to produce that much extra in the future.

Slaves on rice plantations worked on what was called the "task system." They were each responsible for a specific task on the plantation, and once it was completed, they were permitted to spend the rest of the day on their own activities. Masters reasoned that, while slaves in gangs might get away with working at less than full speed, the task laborer was accountable for making sure that he or she completed the assigned work each day. The master's goal in both systems was to achieve greater efficiency and to increase profits.

Railroads

In 1861 the United States had over 30,000 miles (48,000 km) of rail track, just 9,000 miles (13,500 km) of which lay within the South. It was clear to both sides that railroads would play a major role in dictating where their armies would fight.

Curriculum Context

Industrialization had changed the face of warfare; the Civil War has been described as the first industrial war.

Battery

An artillery unit, consisting of a number of guns and their crews.

In August 1861 General George B. McClellan wrote to President Lincoln: "The construction of railroads has introduced a new and very important element into war, by the great facilities thus given for concentrating … large amounts of troops from remote [locations] and by creating a few strategic points and lines of operations." He recommended that the Union army should seize these strategic points on the railroads to stop the Confederates from concentrating their forces. The Confederates had already proved McClellan's point at the Battle of First Bull Run. Warned of an imminent Union advance on the rail center of Manassas Junction, Confederate General Pierre G.T. Beauregard sent trains west to collect reinforcements from the Shenandoah Valley. Within two days over 8,000 infantry and four batteries of artillery had arrived along Bull Run Creek to help meet the Union attack.

As the war went on, troop movements became bigger and took place over greater distances. In July 1862 the Confederate Army of the Mississippi was ordered north from Tupelo, Mississippi, to Chattanooga, Tennessee, a distance of 775 miles (1,250 km). The army traveled by six different railroads, taking a complicated route through Alabama and Georgia, but arrived by the end of the month to allow its commander, Braxton Bragg, to launch an invasion north into Kentucky.

The ability to quickly move entire armies hundreds of miles produced a revolutionary change in warfare. Troops no longer needed to exhaust themselves marching across country, while food and supplies could be delivered where they were needed. The capture of major rail junctions could open up large tracts of enemy territory. The negative side was that armies became dependent on the railroad and had to use thousands of men to protect the lines. An example of this came in June 1862, after Union troops had taken Corinth, Mississippi after their victory at Shiloh. General Ulysses S. Grant's army were stopped from advancing deeper into Mississippi by the need to keep troops in Tennessee to protect the hundreds of miles of railroad that carried all of the army's supplies.

Curriculum Context

A map of the locations of major Civil War battles reveals how important railroad junctions were during the conflict.

The rail gun

One of the many innovations in military technology was the rail gun. Heavy artillery was difficult to move around the battlefield because of its size and weight—a barrel weighing 7,200 pounds (3,265 kg) was not unusual. But in 1862 Confederates fighting the Peninsular Campaign in Virginia had the idea of putting a 32-pound (14.5 kg) siege gun on a flatbed rail truck pushed by a locomotive. The idea worked, and later in 1864, during the Siege of Petersburg, the Union army used a large 13-inch (33 cm) mortar mounted on a train to bombard Confederate positions.

Mortar

A short-barrelled artillery gun designed to fire shells in an arc over enemy defenses.

The U.S. Military Railroad engine *W.H. Whiton*, photographed in 1862. The Railways Act of January 1862 empowered the Union army to commandeer any railroad or rolling stock for the purposes of the war. In practice the law applied mainly to railroads in occupied areas of the South.

Protecting the Railroads

Railroads captured by Union forces in the South then became targets for raids by Confederate cavalry. Raiders such as Nathan Bedford Forrest and John Hunt Morgan could move almost at will in country hostile to the Union, tearing up track, burning bridges, and destroying or stealing supplies. This forced the Union to protect the railroads with blockhouses garrisoned with hundreds of troops. One such blockhouse, attacked by Forrest near Athens, Alabama, in 1864 was a small fort described as "an earthwork 180 by 450 feet [54 by 137 m] surrounded by . . . a palisade 4 feet [1.2 m] high, and a ditch 12 feet [3.6 m] wide." Confederate raiders were not put off by these defenses and in some cases began taking artillery with them to destroy the blockhouses. The fight to control the railroads became a small war of its own.

In the same year the Union army Medical Department developed hospital trains. They were converted passenger cars that had been adapted to move the wounded from field hospitals to hospitals in the North. They were like regular hospitals on rails, with kitchens, dispensaries, and surgeries. The wounded were transported in bunks, and some trains also had racks that could support stretchers.

The Great Locomotive Chase

In April 1862 Union General Ormsby M. Mitchel thought up a plan to capture the city of Chattanooga with a daring raid into Georgia to cut the railroad south from Chattanooga to Atlanta, making it impossible for Confederate reinforcements to reach the city.

A Union spy, James J. Andrews, was to lead the raid, with 24 Union soldiers dressed in civilian clothes and armed only with revolvers. The soldiers were to rendezvous with Andrews in Marietta, Georgia, over 200 miles (320 km) behind enemy lines. There they would board a train heading for Chattanooga, hijack it, and travel north, destroying rail lines, cutting telegraph wires, and burning bridges.

Curriculum Context

Andrews is an example of an individual who, although not a military commander, might possibly have altered the course of the war.

The raiders met at Marietta as planned and boarded a north-bound mail train pulled by the locomotive *General*. At the town of Big Shanty a few miles up the line the train stopped, and the conductor, engineer, and passengers got off to have breakfast. Running forward, Andrews and three others uncoupled most of the cars. The party took possession of the locomotive and started the train moving. Confederate guards could only stand and stare as the train rolled away.

Journey of destruction

Andrews' journey of destruction had begun, but he was soon being pursued. Two men, a mechanic named Murphy and the conductor of the hijacked train, W.A. Fuller, gave chase. At first they had to follow on foot, but they soon found a handcar and reached Etowah Station. There Fuller took over an old locomotive called the *Yonah*, loaded it with troops, and set off in pursuit.

Andrews meanwhile was bluffing his way down the line by explaining that the *General* was pulling an ammunition train. But news of the stolen train was spreading, and Fuller and Murphy were only four minutes behind. Andrews now ordered more track to be destroyed. Murphy and Fuller again gave chase on foot. Soon they found another train, commandeered it, and set off at high speed with more soldiers.

The Yankees tried to lay obstacles on the line, but the Confederates were still gaining and were soon within rifle range. Andrews hoped to destroy the rail bridges south of Chattanooga; but Fuller and Murphy were too close behind, and the *General* was running out of fuel. Andrews accepted defeat and ordered his men to jump from the train and try to escape back to Union lines. The raid had failed, and the plan was canceled. The raiders were captured. Since they were dressed as civilians, Andrews and seven others were executed as spies, while the rest were imprisoned.

Handcar
A small railroad car powered by raising and lowering a rocking arm.

Commandeer
To seize private goods for military purposes.

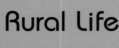

Rural Life

Rural life during the 19th-century in the United States was hard, since farmwork was largely carried out by hand. The Civil War years saw the start of the first U.S. agricultural revolution, as horse power began to take over from hand power.

Curriculum Context

Some curricula expect students to be familiar with the development of agrarian society in the United States, particularly in contrast to that of industrial society.

Curriculum Context

The influence of mechanized farming is also important for students studying the postwar period.

There were over two million farms in the United States in 1860, and 58 percent of Americans worked in agriculture. Recent technological advances had changed rural life. Kerosene lamps, which became widespread in the early 1860s, brought better lighting to rural homes. The growing railroad network brought farmers new markets.

Most Civil War soldiers were farmers or the sons of farmers. While they were fighting, their mothers, wives, and daughters found themselves responsible for all farm activities, not just traditional women's tasks such as raising poultry and preserving food. The Civil War challenged farmers to increase food production to feed both soldiers and civilians. High crop prices and a shortage of farmworkers encouraged Northern farmers to adopt mechanized equipment to reduce the amount of manual work and increase production.

New inventions

In 1833 the mechanical reaper was developed to cut grain, a task previously done by hand. At the start of war around 70 percent of the wheat raised west of the Appalachians was harvested mechanically. Wartime labor shortages encouraged grain farmers to use improved reapers. Manufacturers made 85,000 reapers in 1864: more than the total between 1833 and 1861. When the war began, reapers had crews of eight to ten men, who could harvest 10–12 acres (4–4.8 ha) per day. Improvements meant that by the end of the war, eight men could harvest 15 acres (6 ha) per day.

The success of the mechanized reaper encouraged the development of other implements, such as grain drills, horse-powered threshing machines, and riding plows. The improvements reduced the worker-hours required to produce 1 acre (0.4 ha) of wheat from 35 to 20. This allowed Northern farmers to feed civilians and soldiers and even to export food. The United States exported 27 million bushels of wheat annually in the war years, a big increase from the 8 million bushels exported annually during the 1850s. New canning technology improved the preservation of fruits and vegetables, while Gail Borden's new method of preserving milk by condensing it and canning it expanded the market and improved nutrition.

Rural life in the South

In the South farmers had limited access to new technology. The Confederate government wanted manufacturers to produce weapons, not agricultural tools. Cotton still had to be picked by hand, because no one had developed a mechanical way of harvesting the crop. Many plantation owners resisted the adoption of new tools that would remove the need for slave labor, in which they had invested their money. Replacement parts and new tools became increasingly scarce during the war as equipment wore out or was destroyed where the armies fought.

Different outcomes

Farmers in the North increased agricultural production with the aid of improved technology for the market economy and for domestic use. Southern farmers struggled to grow food crops, rather than cotton, to feed their soldiers and civilians. When the war ended in 1865, Northern agriculture had undergone great change in the form of technological adoption and an increasing dependence on the market economy, while Southern farmers and planters suffered from a lack of technological change and the loss of slave labor.

Schools and Education

On the eve of the Civil War Americans were among the best educated in the world. In parts of the most highly educated region, New England, 90 percent of adults could read and write, and 75 percent of children attended school.

Curriculum Context

Many curricula expect students to be able to describe the development of the public school system in the United States.

In many Northern states a system of public education had been established in the 1830s. Common schools, the forerunners of today's public schools, existed alongside private schools, charity schools, and Christian schools. Children who did not attend school during the working week could learn basic literacy at Sunday schools. In frontier areas children attended small one-room schoolhouses or were educated by their parents.

The situation was less positive in the South, where only 80 percent of the white population was literate. One-third of Southern white children were enrolled in school, but the labor demands of the rural economy meant that on average they attended for only three months a year. Lower educational standards in the South resulted in a less literary culture. In 1860 the North published three times as many copies of newspapers per person than did the South, and the South produced and sold fewer books than the North.

Curriculum Context

Many families relied on children to help on the farm, which they thought was more important than going to school.

Attitudes to education

Many Southerners belittled Yankee faith in education. They argued that universal schooling was not only impractical; it was actually inappropriate in a society that was largely made up of subsistence farmers with little need to read or write. In the prewar period an article in the *Southern Review*, a South Carolina newspaper, explained, "To make every child in the state a literary character would not be a good qualification for those who must live by manual labor."

Across the Northern states, with the exception of Massachusetts, black and white children were educated separately. State funding of schools for blacks was patchy and often reliant on charitable donations. In New York, for example, the New York Manumission Society organized special "Negro schools" as part of the system of public instruction. The local school boards were white-controlled, and educational funding for blacks rarely compared to that for white children. Black schools were usually poorly heated and furnished, and lacked books and other basic educational materials. There were a few "Negro colleges" in the Northern states. Most were the result of private benevolence, such as Avery College in Pittsburgh, which had been established in 1849 by abolitionist Charles Avery with a fund of $300,000.

An illustration from *Harper's Weekly* of December 1866, showing a school for black children in Charleston, South Carolina, run by the Freedman's Aid Society. A number of black schools were set up in the South during the Civil War by voluntary organizations.

Changing attitudes

Attitudes toward the Northern black population changed during the war, and in many states this was reflected in better funding for black education after the war. In 1865 Rhode Island followed the example of Massachusetts and desegregated its schools. In 1867 Connecticut also began to educate black and white children together. However, progress was slow, and in many states schools remained segregated until the end of the century.

In the South some education was offered to slaves liberated by Union troops, but it was provided mostly by voluntary organizations. Many Negro schools operating under government auspices were actually run by the Freedman's Aid organizations. In the postwar era Southern education was strictly segregated, with funding for blacks well below that for whites.

Impact of the war

In practical terms schools in the North were little affected by the war, although older pupils did leave to work in the fields or the factories, and a wartime shortage of male teachers accelerated the trend toward female domination of the teaching profession. The impact of war on schools in the South was far greater. They suffered from falling rolls as parents diverted school fees to more urgent priorities, and older children replaced their fathers in the fields.

Schoolteachers were exempt from conscription, but many signed up, and an influx of draft dodgers was not enough to prevent shortages. Many Confederate schools closed or shortened their semesters. Higher education institutions also suffered from falling rolls as students enlisted. Many never returned to their studies. Schools also served as useful propaganda forums on both sides of the Mason–Dixon line.

Desegregation

Stopping the practice of separating people on the basis of their race.

Propaganda

Material intended to make its observers support a particular cause, often by providing a biased account of the facts.

Slaves' Education

Before the war the education of the slave population in the South was positively discouraged, and teaching slaves to read was illegal in several states. Slaveholders believed that if their slaves were taught to read, they would read abolitionist material, which might provoke insurrection and revolt. A slave owner from Tennessee explained to his Northern relatives in 1859 that he did not educate his slaves because "It would do them no good. They were not like white folks. If they could read it would only make them discontented and put bad ideas in their heads."

Despite such attitudes, around one in 10 slaves in the South did gain basic literacy skills. They learned how to read and write from free blacks, from other slaves, or from a minority of benevolent whites. Evangelical Christians were especially likely to defy the law and teach their slaves to read the scriptures. That was because evangelical religion placed a high value on personal religious experience and revelation, which were only possible if believers were able to read the Bible for themselves rather than relying on priests to read it for them.

Sense of identity

Education in the North, even outside of the Sunday schools, was deeply imbued with Protestant ethics. *The New England Primer*, a reading book that included such sentences as "In Adam's Fall, we sinned all," was popular throughout the Union. Children were also taught about the U.S. government. They memorized the federal catechism (a series of questions and answers about the Constitution) from *Webster's American Spelling Book*. In the South school textbooks stressed Confederate virtue and Yankee wrongdoing. Children were encouraged to see themselves and their studies as vital to the survival of the Confederacy. Ideas taught in school classrooms in the North and South helped create patriotic identities for the Union and the Confederacy.

Protestant ethics

A short-hand term for a view of the world that emphasizes hard work, ethics, and sober and modest behavior.

Curriculum Context

You might be asked to identify lasting effects of the Civil War.

Smuggling and Piracy

Faced with a strangling Union blockade and with no powerful navy of its own, the Confederacy turned to individuals to help beat the blockade and damage Union merchant shipping. The Union accused it of smuggling and piracy.

Curriculum Context

The long coastline of the South proved a formidable challenge for the U.S. vessels enforcing the blockade.

The blockade involved Union warships patrolling the South's long coastline to prevent merchant vessels leaving from or entering Confederate ports. To enforce the blockade, President Abraham Lincoln had to press into service all available ships, including much of the U.S. Revenue Marine Fleet. As a result, only a few ships were left to combat smuggling in the North, an activity that increased considerably during the conflict as taxes were imposed on luxury goods to help finance the war.

Running the blockade

The Union government condemned all Confederate attempts to circumvent the blockade as smuggling, but for the South they were an essential means of obtaining supplies and equipment for the war effort. Smuggling goods through the blockade—blockade-running—required fast ships and courageous captains. Many blockade-runners were British, although the best known was probably the Virginian Lieutenant John Wilkinson (1821–1891), who commanded the CSS *Robert E. Lee*.

Curriculum Context

The motives of the blockade-runners might be an interesting topic for investigation.

The risks of blockade-running meant that huge profits could be made. Many captains were motivated by the chance to make money, although patriotism also played a part. The Confederate government was forced to commission a fleet of blockade-runners directly so they could make the crews import essential war supplies. Otherwise captains tended to carry luxury goods such as brandy and silk, which were more profitable than bulky war supplies such as iron.

Despite the best efforts of the Union navy, it was unable to enforce the blockade completely. For example, smugglers in Florida did a brisk trade exporting cattle to Cuba in exchange for gold coins and other supplies. The smugglers' knowledge of the southwest Florida coast, which was dotted with dozens of islands, meant they were able to escape capture time and again.

Piracy or privateering?

On April 17, 1861, Confederate President Jefferson Davis announced he would issue "letters of marque" to private armed ships. These documents allowed captains to capture Union merchant ships at sea. The privateers would split the profits on the captured ship and cargo with the Confederate government. One aim of the policy was to destroy the blockade by forcing the Union to deploy its ships to chase privateers rather than enforcing the blockade. Privateering had worked well for the United States during the American Revolution and the War of 1812. However, in 1856 European countries had signed the Declaration of Paris abolishing privateering. Now President Abraham Lincoln declared that all privateers would be regarded as pirates and would be hanged if caught.

Privateer

A pirate given a government license to attack enemy ships and seize their cargo.

The Bahamas

Many people in the Bahamas were prepared to defy the Union blockade and continue to trade with the South. The economy of the islands boomed during the war. The community of West End on Grand Bahama Island, for example, had been in decline for many years, but during the war its population doubled. Its boom was entirely due to smuggling. Only 55 miles (88 km) from the coast of the Confederacy, Bahamians were ideally placed to take full advantage of the Civil War. They took cotton from blockade-runners, selling it on to English mills to be woven into cloth. In return, traders on the islands sold guns and ammunition to the munitions-starved Confederates. They could command high prices and became rich very quickly.

The Confederate privateer *Petrel* being sunk by the Union frigate USS *St. Lawrence* in 1861. The *Petrel*, formerly the Union revenue cutter USS *Aiken*, had been seized earlier in the year by the Confederacy along with six other Union cutters, all of which were then converted into privateers.

Privateers had their heyday in 1861. They succeeded in wreaking damage on the North's merchant fleet, intercepting Union vessels as far away as the English Channel, Cape Horn, and even Australia.

However, as the Union blockade took hold in 1862, it became increasingly difficult to bring captured vessels into Confederate ports, which was necessary for the privateer captain to claim his profits. Overall, privateers had little effect on the actual outcome of the war in comparison to the Confederate "commerce raiders" that preyed on Union merchant shipping.

Commerce raider

A Confederate ship that targeted Union merchant shipping in order to undermine the North's ability to trade.

Customs controls

Less dramatic, but equally important to the North, was the work of customs officials, who were charged with blocking the movement of cargo bound for Southern ports, either from the North or from foreign ports.

Baltimore, Maryland, became a smuggling center. It had long been a major transfer point for goods between North and South. In addition, many of its citizens were Southern sympathizers. Plenty of people in the North were only too prepared to smuggle contraband goods into the South—more often than not because smuggling could be very profitable.

Trade

In both the Union and the Confederacy trade played an important role in determining the outcome of the Civil War. Types of trade included internal domestic trade, trade with foreign countries, and even trade with the enemy.

Before the Civil War the United States had become one of the world's leading commercial economies. The major countries of Europe, particularly Britain, had launched their industrial revolutions in the 1700s, with the cotton textile industry becoming their most important industry. The northeastern United States had also industrialized in the decades leading up to the Civil War. Southern plantations supplied raw cotton to both Northern and European factories, bringing great prosperity to the slave-based economy of the Deep South. The states of the Midwest became major food producers, exporting their crops of wheat and corn to both the Northeast and Europe. The vitality of the U.S. economy depended heavily on trade among the various regions of the country and on trade between the United States and Europe.

Cotton is King!

Some Southerners believed the South's near-monopoly on the supply of cotton would give them the power either to prevent a war or to win one. South Carolina's Senator James Henry Hammond addressing the North warned, "You dare not make war on cotton. No power on earth dares to make war upon it. Cotton is king!" In keeping with this, the Confederate government in 1861 decided to halve cotton exports to Great Britain. Since Britain imported 80 percent of its cotton from the South, Jefferson Davis and his advisers hoped their action would cripple Britain's economy, force it to recognize the Confederacy as independent and to provide aid, perhaps even siding with the Confederacy.

Failure of the cotton embargo

The plan did not work. First, the large cotton crops of 1859 and 1860 meant Britain still had a surplus so the cut in trade had little immediate effect. Britain was already developing alternative sources of cotton in Egypt and India. They would soon replace the South as Britain's major source of cotton. Finally, Confederate leaders underestimated how much Britain depended on imports of food from the North. Its dependence grew dramatically in the early years of the war after a series of crop failures in Europe. Union exports of wheat to Europe grew from 17 million bushels in 1860 to 58 million in 1863, and other food exports such as corn, pork, and beef increased similarly. By 1863 Britain was buying between one-third to one-half of its food from the United States. Faced with the choice between Confederate cotton or Union wheat, they chose wheat.

Lacking the factories of the Union, the Confederacy had to import much of the arms, clothing, medicine, and other supplies necessary to fight the war. The Union government therefore imposed a naval blockade around the entire Southern coastline from Virginia to Texas. The Confederacy responded by encouraging the construction and purchase of blockade-runners, fast steamships that could outrun the Union blockading fleet and conduct trade in and out of Confederate ports. Many of these ships were built in foreign shipyards, particularly in Britain.

At the beginning of the war the blockade was not very effective; it has been estimated that in 1861 nine out of every ten blockade-runners managed to get through the Union blockade. But the Confederacy's ability to replace vessels that were caught was limited, and by 1865 only half the ships were successfully running the blockade. The result for the Confederacy was chronic shortages of many necessary goods and a reduced ability to wage war.

A crowd of people wait in the square of a Southern town to take the oath of allegiance to the Union after the end of the Civil War. After taking the oath, citizens were granted a number of privileges, including the right to open a shop to trade in rations supplied from military stores.

Britain's stance

The British government issued a proclamation of neutrality in May 1861, meaning they could trade with both sides. Most historians believe this policy benefited the Union more than the Confederacy. The Confederate government continued to hope battle successes would persuade the British to change their minds and recognize the Confederacy. Those hopes faded after the Emancipation Proclamation came into effect and vanished when the war turned in favor of the Union after the battles of Vicksburg and Gettysburg.

At first the Confederate government allowed privately owned blockade-runners to import and export whatever goods their owners wished (except for cotton, the export ban on which was only lifted in 1863). This became a problem because ship owners discovered that importing luxury items brought higher profits than war necessities. Confederacy and individual state governments began to outfit their own blockade-runners and stipulated that private runners reserve one-third of their cargo space for military-related goods. These measures were inadequate, and in early 1864 the government outlawed the importation of all luxuries and increased the cargo space that had to be reserved for military goods to 50 percent.

With the ban on cotton exports lifted, the Confederacy eventually exported a total of about one million bales during the last three years of the war, but this was small compared with the 10 million bales shipped in the three years before the war. The Union blockade reduced exports from the Confederacy to less than a third of their prewar levels.

Trading with the enemy

Both the Union and the Confederacy outlawed trade with the enemy at the start of the war, but there were always ways around it. Much trade was conducted in secret, goods even being smuggled through army lines. However, the U.S. Congress also allowed Confederates to trade with Unionists in parts of the Confederacy that came under Union occupation— Southern planters or merchants had to swear an oath of allegiance to the Union in order to trade. There were several reasons for this policy. It was a way to win the allegiance of former Confederates; it helped restore the economies of occupied areas; and it furnished much-needed food and supplies to Union troops, who might otherwise have to rely on supply lines from the North.

Corruption and profiteering

The Union policy could be counterproductive. Money paid to local merchants and planters often found its way back into the Confederate treasury. There was widespread corruption and profiteering within the Union military as they traded with the enemy in violation of their rules. The problem was especially bad in New Orleans and Memphis, two major Southern commercial centers that had been occupied by Union forces early in the war. The South sold as much cotton to the North as it did to Europe. On balance, trading with the enemy probably did more damage to the Union than it did to the Confederacy. The Union could have survived without the money and goods but for the Confederacy, such trade became a necessity.

Profiteering

To make unreasonably high profits by selling essential goods at high prices during times of emergency, such as wars.

Curriculum Context

Should the Union have simply halted all trade with the Confederacy, or did it benefit from the practice?

Impact on North and South

Historians continue to debate whether the Civil War was positive or negative for the Northern economy. The production, sales, and exports of cotton textiles declined, but companies involved in the manufacture and trade of war-related goods flourished. Farmers had profitable contracts to supply the Union army; and the growth in foreign demand meant that the Union produced more wheat in 1862 than the whole nation had in 1859. Ship-building boomed, as the Union navy grew from 42 ships in 1861 to 671 by 1865. The volume of goods carried by Northern railroads doubled.

It was a different story in the Confederacy. The blockade, unwise government policies, and setbacks on the battlefield dampened public confidence. The economy floundered, and the Confederate dollar was hit by severe inflation. The prices the government paid for food and supplies lagged behind the market price, so merchants and farmers often refused to sell. Finally, the Confederate Congress passed the Impressment Act of 1863, which allowed authorities to seize goods they needed and leave behind a government I.O.U. Unlike in the North, Southerners all too often felt robbed by their government. In trade, then, the Union enjoyed advantages over the South that in the long run helped bring about the defeat of the Confederacy.

> **Curriculum Context**
>
> The rapid economic development of the North greatly influenced the United States' emergence as a world power in the late 19th century.

> **Impressment**
>
> The compulsory seizing of goods by governments for public use.

The Confederate cruiser CSS *Sumter* runs the Union blockade of the port of St. Pierre on Martinique in the West Indies in November 1861. The *Sumter* succeeded in reaching the port to unload its cargo and take on board goods badly needed by the Confederacy.

Transportation

Efficient transportation systems were essential to the conduct of the Civil War. Armies of tens of thousands of men were fighting over vast areas and needed to be moved and supplied with arms, food, and equipment.

Curriculum Context

Curricula might expect students to understand the importance of rivers as transportation links, particularly in the center and west of the continent.

Most Civil War battles and campaigns were fought for control of the river and rail networks. Confederate cavalry began raids on railroads used by the Union in Virginia within days of the start of the war, while half of the Union war effort from 1861 to 1863 was devoted to gaining control of the Mississippi River.

Large-scale transportation

Major campaigns depended on efficient large-scale transportation. Large numbers of men and supplies were usually transported by train or vessels known as transports. Union General George B. McClellan's Peninsular Campaign in spring 1862 depended on hundreds of transports to move his army from the Potomac River down Chesapeake Bay to the James River. Transports were also vital to Union General Ulysses S. Grant's success at Vicksburg in 1863. In order to attack the city, he first ferried his army by river boat across to the east bank of the Mississippi. The Confederates never built enough transports to control the rivers and so relied more heavily on the railroads.

Curriculum Context

The Civil War proved the usefulness of railroads in warfare; when World War I broke out in 1914, the German war plan depended entirely on moving troops by train.

Rail transportation

The importance of the rail networks was shown as early as July 1861, when Confederate reinforcements were transported to the battlefield at the Battle of First Bull Run (Manassas). The Southern states had only 9,000 miles (14,400 km) of track compared to 21,000 miles (33,600 km) in the North. Southern railroads were run by different companies using different gauges (widths) of track. They helped transport troops, but at a price. It was only in March 1865 that President Jefferson Davis brought the railroads and steamboats under control of the Confederate War Department, by which time the South was near defeat. The Confederate army managed to use the railroads to good effect, especially for transporting men over the large areas necessary to fight in the western theater. In March 1862 General Albert S. Johnston assembled an army of 40,000 men at the rail junction at Corinth, Mississippi with regiments from as far as Louisiana and Alabama. Three months later Confederate General Braxton Bragg moved the Army of Mississippi 776 miles (1,242 km) by rail from Tupelo, Mississippi, to Chattanooga, Tennessee for an offensive north into Kentucky. It took three weeks and six separate rail lines to move 25,000 men.

Curriculum Context

More than in the East, the war in the West was conducted over great distances.

New transport systems

Armies had their own transportation systems to keep them supplied on campaign. The Army of the Potomac's invasion of Virginia in May 1864 was supplied by a wagon train 5 miles (8 km) long that

The Union transport *Chattanooga* loaded with supplies for the Army of the Cumberland in 1863.

followed the troops. During the Siege of Petersburg, Virginia, later that year, the Union army supplemented its supplies from transports that steamed up the James River. Supplies arriving by river were distributed by rail from the Union supply depot at City Point.

Transport disaster

In April 1865, shortly after the war ended, a disaster occurred on a Union transport on the Mississippi River. The *Sultana*, a side-wheeled steamboat, was carrying more than 2,000 released Union prisoners of war from Vicksburg north to Cairo, Illinois. The vessel was overloaded with passengers; and on the night of the 27th, near Memphis, a boiler exploded and the steamer sank, killing about 1,700 people. The sinking of the *Sultana* was the worst maritime disaster in U.S. history.

Curriculum Context

Students might be asked to describe the influence of the *Sultana* disaster on later safety legislation.

The First Ambulances

At the end of 1862 the Union army created a system for transporting wounded men off the battlefield. At the insistence of William A. Hammond, the surgeon general, an ambulance system was established under the Medical Department. It was responsible for transporting wounded men to regimental aid posts, from there to field hospitals in the rear, and then to base hospitals in Northern cities. The system was a great success. After the Battle of Fredericksburg in December 1862 the medical director of VI Corps praised the work of the ambulances in his report: "Two hours after the engagement such was the celerity [swiftness] ... with which the ambulances worked, the whole number of wounded [about 800] were within hospitals under the care of nurses." On July 4, 1863, the day after the Battle of Gettysburg ended, not one of the 14,500 injured Union soldiers remained on the battlefield.

The Union army's medical transportation system included horse-drawn ambulances, hospital trains, and converted steamboats used as hospital boats. Some hospital trains were freight cars padded with straw bedding, while others were fully converted hospitals complete with dispensaries and surgeries. The steamboats were taken from the army's Quartermaster Department, converted into floating field hospitals, and placed under the control of army surgeons. One vessel on the Tennessee River housed a thousand wounded men after the Battle of Shiloh in April 1862, while another is recorded to have transported more than 12,000 wounded in a year.

Urban Life

During the war civilians tried to maintain as much normality in their lives as the conflict allowed. In the big cities the effects of war on day-to-day life were complex and differed widely between the Union and the Confederacy.

In 1860 one-quarter of Northerners lived in towns and cities. With the exception of Washington, D.C, and Philadelphia on the eve of the Battle of Gettysburg in July 1863, none of the great Northern cities was ever in imminent danger of assault. For citizens of New York, Boston, and Chicago the war was a long way away. Life was very different for the one-tenth of Southerners living in urban areas. In Richmond, the Confederate capital, war was always close by. Cities along the Mississippi River, such as Nashville, Vicksburg, and New Orleans, were under Union occupation by 1863. By that time Northern cities were seeing an unprecedented economic boom, bringing prosperity to many.

Curriculum Context

Students might be asked to contrast the experiences of city dwellers in the North and in the South.

Tensions in New York

There were exceptions. During the war New York was embroiled in controversy that often spilled into violence. During the draft riot of July 1863 police lost control of the city, and rioters killed hundreds of people. Behind the incident lay tensions and hatreds that already existed and were inflamed by the war. One-quarter of the city's 800,000 inhabitants were Irish immigrants, most uneducated and unskilled. They lived in slums in lower Manhattan and worked at menial jobs, such as street paving and dockside labor. Poor blacks lived alongside them competing for the same jobs. The Irish found an outlet for their frustrations by directing their venom at blacks. The last thing they wanted to do was fight a war on behalf of people they thought inferior. The draft riot was an expression of Irish anger and resentment at the whole situation.

Curriculum Context

The cities of the North were full of divisions and tensions between ethnic and religious groups.

A skating carnival held in Brooklyn, New York City, on February 10, 1862. Life in most Northern cities went on much as usual during the Civil War.

At the same time, the Irish and other poor Northerners felt—with good reason—that the draft was unfair since it allowed the better-off to buy their way out of the army. Northern city-dwellers with money felt no disgrace in hiring a substitute to fight for them or paying an exemption fee. That left them free to carry on with their lives as though there were no war. The gap between rich and poor grew as wartime inflation grew and the huge profits made by wealthy financiers who traded in war supplies increased. For all these reasons the mood of many people on the streets of New York, and to a lesser extent in other cities of the Union, was often surly and defensive.

Conditions in Washington

In Washington, D.C., daily life was conducted with the war right on the doorstep. From the First Battle of Bull Run in July 1861 until July 1864, when a corps of the Army of Northern Virginia had the capital in its sights, Washington was braced for invasion. The city was a military encampment, with soldiers everywhere, and makeshift field hospitals strung out along the Mall, where many of Washington's women rolled up their sleeves and tended the casualties. The capital, which was built on swampy land and became swelteringly

Curriculum Context

It might be interesting to investigate how the war impacted on the lives of civilians in the capital, Washington, D.C.

hot in summer, had never been considered a healthy place to live. During the war the concentration of sick and wounded men meant that disease was rife throughout the city. Maintaining even basic standards of hygiene proved impossible under such conditions.

Life in the South

Life in Southern cities became very difficult during the war. The Union blockade of Southern ports starved the South of imports, and along with runaway inflation, living standards fell for everybody. With virtually every able-bodied white man of military age away fighting, great burdens fell on women's shoulders. Richmond ladies, who had lived in luxury, were reduced to cutting up their fine gowns from Paris and selling them in small pieces to be made into bonnets to put basic food on the table. Despite so many privations, Confederate city dwellers accepted it was necessary to make sacrifices for the war effort. This was in contrast to the Union, where many people were lukewarm or opposed to the war. The most serious flareup of discontent in the Confederacy occurred in April 1863, when a mob in Richmond went on a rampage demanding bread. Clothing and jewelry stores were looted, as well as bakeries and food stores.

Inflation

Prices in the South rose by as much as 9,000 percent.

Curriculum Context

What does Southerners' willingness to make sacrifices reveal about the relative motivations of the two sides in the war?

Occupation of New Orleans

New Orleans had an unusual experience of the war because it was captured by the Union army very early, in the spring of 1862. The occupying authority was vested in General Benjamin F. Butler—"Beast" Butler, as the citizens of New Orleans referred to him. His chief crime in their eyes was his lack of chivalry toward the city's women. At the beginning of the occupation some of them showed their contempt for Union soldiers by emptying chamber pots over their heads from upstairs windows or spitting at them as they passed by. Butler provoked outrage by passing a decree that a women who displayed discourtesy to Union soldiers would be dealt with as common prostitutes. In late 1862 Butler was replaced by General Nathaniel P. Banks, who proved a less controversial military commander. Union military occupation of the city continued until March 1866.

Women

The Civil War was not waged by armies alone. Entire communities, North and South, were mobilized to back the war effort, and that meant women played a much larger role in the conflict than in previous wars.

Curriculum Context

In order to judge how women's roles were changed by the war, it is important to appreciate their traditional place in society and in the family.

In 1861 few Americans, male or female, questioned the idea that politics and war were a man's business. Men and women occupied separate social roles to which each sex was thought suited. Women (white, middle-class women, at least) stayed in the home, where they kept house and raised children. In the United States of the 19th century women were thought to possess superior moral qualities to men, which made them well suited to giving religious instruction to children and keeping virtuous households. Men were free to venture out into the rough-and-tumble worlds of business and politics, knowing when they returned home a well-ordered, nurturing environment awaited them.

The home front

When the war began, most women did their bit for the war effort from home or in church groups. Union and Confederate women made bandages, knitted socks and blankets, and sewed shirts, pants, and underwear to be sent to the soldiers at the front. They wrote encouraging letters to absent husbands, brothers, and sons. Women willingly spent time and money doing things they believed would help the war effort and shorten the length of their separation from loved ones.

Curriculum Context

The temperance and abolition movements were often also related with the movement for women suffrage. Why might that be the case?

Unexpected consequence

Assigning superior moral and religious qualities to women meant that, particularly in the North, women traditionally got involved in church work and in various reform organizations such as the temperance (anti-alcohol) and abolition movements. As guardians of society's religion and morality, women became leaders in these movements, which frequently took them from the home. Many Northern women entered the war more prepared than their Southern sisters to help the war effort outside the home.

Voluntary organizations

The first voluntary organizations were soldiers' aid societies, local groups organized by women to raise funds and collect food, clothing, and medical supplies for the soldiers. Thousands of organizations sprang up in the North. In the Confederacy the movement was slower, but by 1862 such groups had become common.

Northern women began to see the need for a central organization to coordinate relief efforts. In New York City on April 29, 1861, Elizabeth Blackwell, the first

Curriculum Context

What factors might have made Southern women slower to work together in organized societies?

Men's Work

For every woman who served as a nurse or a worker in an official relief society there were hundreds who contributed to the war effort in an unofficial capacity by keeping the economy going. In both the Union and Confederacy, as thousands of men departed for the armies, rural women left the household and began working in the fields to keep their families and the armies fed. In the North the absence of men increased the use of mechanized equipment on farms, enabling women to keep agricultural production at a rate nearly equal to the prewar level. On the slave plantations of the Confederacy the wives of slaveholders began from necessity to carry out the duties of the previously all-male occupation of overseer, supervising the work of slaves whose agricultural labor kept Confederate armies in the field supplied with food.

Women also moved into the ranks of industrial workers in unprecedented numbers. In the North before the war women already worked in certain industries, especially textiles and shoemaking. The numbers of women in such industries steadily increased during the war. Because they were generally paid much less than men in the same jobs, their presence helped keep inflation low, which in turn aided the Union war effort. Women also went to work in munitions factories and government agencies, another first. The United States Treasury Department gave jobs to more than 400 female clerks, the Confederate treasury employed perhaps half that many.

A drawing by Alfred Waud of a female sutler with her cart selling provisions to soldiers at the front. Sutlers were civilians who followed the armies and sold items such as food, tobacco, newspapers, and tin plates to the troops.

American woman to graduate from medical school and become a licensed doctor, called a meeting to organize the Women's Central Association for Relief (WCAR). Its task was to create a training program for nurses.

Nursing the wounded

It took the intervention of the Secretary of War Simon Cameron and President Abraham Lincoln, for their ideas to be taken seriously. On June 13, 1861, Lincoln signed an order creating the United States Sanitary Commission, a voluntary organization that would work closely with the Union government and army to improve the health and medical treatment of Union troops. By the end of the war some 3,200 women had served in hospitals as Union nurses.

Nursing on the front line

At first, female nurses could only serve in base hospitals behind the lines, where soldiers were brought for longer-term care. But soon women began appearing in the makeshift hospitals in the army camps. Some, like Clara Barton, who would later found the American Red Cross, worked on or near the front lines. When a major battle took place near a town or city, such as the 1863 Battle of Gettysburg, local women opened their homes to the wounded and became instant amateur nurses.

The Confederacy was slower to allow female nurses to treat the sick and wounded. Nevertheless, by the summer of 1862 individual Southern women were volunteering to serve in Confederate hospitals. In September 1862 the Confederate Congress passed a law allowing female nurses to work in army hospitals, something that was unthinkable before the war. The Confederate army also used many slave women in more menial jobs in hospitals and army camps.

Spies and soldiers

In both the Union and the Confederacy a few daring women sought to participate directly in the military effort as spies and even as soldiers. In Washington, D.C., the wealthy socialite Rose O'Neal Greenhow ran a Confederate spy ring in the first year of the war. At the First Battle of Bull Run (Battle of Manassas, July 21, 1861), Greenhow is said to have alerted Confederate General Pierre G.T. Beauregard to the advance of Union General Irvin McDowell's army, helping give the Confederates time to bring up reinforcements and win the battle. In his 1862 campaign in the Shenandoah Valley Confederate General Thomas J. "Stonewall" Jackson was helped by Southern spy Belle Boyd, who kept him informed of Union troop movements.

On the Union side one of the most famous female spies was Mary Edwards Walker, a physician who in 1864 was an assistant surgeon in the 52nd Ohio Infantry. Walker crossed Confederate lines to treat the wounded of both sides, while gathering military intelligence. She was captured by the Confederacy and later released in a prisoner exchange. After the war President Andrew Johnson awarded her the Medal of Honor.

If women wanted a more direct part in the fighting, they had to pose as men. Historians estimate that between 500 and 1,000 women, disguised as men, enlisted in both armies; more served on the Union side.

Curriculum Context

You might be asked to evaluate the contribution made to the progress of the war by espionage and intelligence; the First Battle of Bull Run might be a good example to study.

Medal of Honor
The Medal of Honor was created by Abraham Lincoln in 1862 to be awarded to military personnel for displays of outstanding gallantry in the Civil War.

Female Fighters

Few of the female soldiers who disguised themselves as men to serve in the armies proved unfit for duty. Most whose true identity was discovered during the war were exposed only after being captured, wounded, or falling ill. Some, like Mrs. S. M. Blaylock of the Confederacy's 26th North Carolina Infantry, who voluntarily disclosed her gender after her husband was discharged, served for only a short period of time. Others, like an Irish immigrant known only by her male name of Albert D.J. Cashier, served for virtually the entire war. Cashier fought in the 95th Illinois Infantry for three full years and participated in some 40 battles, leaving only when her regiment was disbanded in August 1865. Cashier, like many others, applied for and received a government pension for her service after the war. Female soldiers were not numerous enough to have had any real effect on the outcome of any battles, but their presence in the ranks proves some women felt strongly enough, and were brave enough, to face both the risk of death or injury during battle and the risk of ridicule if their masquerade were discovered.

Curriculum Context

Women are allowed to serve in the U.S. Army today; should they have been allowed to serve openly in the Civil War?

Keeping their secret

Women enlistees used a variety of ingenious disguises, and under the pressure to meet enlistment quotas recruitment officers usually gave volunteers only the briefest questioning before approving them for service. In some cases fellow soldiers may have learned of their comrades' gender only after the women had proved themselves as valuable soldiers, and so they may have conspired with them to keep the secret.

Historians have found a variety of motives for the women's actions. Frances Hook and her brother were orphans; when he joined the Union army, she went along too. After she was wounded and taken prisoner, her captors discovered she was a woman and released her in a prisoner exchange. Others, like Satronia Smith Hunt of an Iowa regiment, enlisted to be with their husbands. Some women joined out of a spirit of adventure, patriotism, or a combination of the two. The cash bounties paid to volunteers probably also influenced the decisions of some poor women to enlist.

Prisoner exchange

An organized swap of prisoners of war performed by both sides.

Enduring hardship

The hardships and horrors of the war, especially in the Confederacy, often brought about a change of attitude in the later stages of the conflict. Confederate women grew to resent their government. As Confederate money became nearly worthless and shortages of food and other necessities became severe, many women began to question whether the war was fair or right. In April 1863 an angry mob of Confederate women marched to the government commissary in the capital demanding bread. Only when President Jefferson Davis threatened to have troops open fire did the mob disperse. Davis urged farmers to plant only food crops, but such scenes became increasingly common as the military and economic fortunes of the Confederacy worsened drastically.

Historians still debate the extent the Civil War brought changes to the lives of women. A number of new work opportunities—as nurses, teachers, factory workers— were opened. The larger movement for women's rights was strengthened by the experience of war. But after the war most women in the South, and to a lesser degree in the North, resumed their prewar roles as housewives and mothers. The world of business and politics remained a male domain for decades to come.

Commissary

A storehouse of goods and provisions for military use.

Curriculum Context

Students may be asked to evaluate the Civil War as a significant step in the history of women's changing position in society.

A woman with her three children posing in front of a tent with her soldier husband, with other soldiers in the background. Families often followed their menfolk to the war, the women acting as cooks, laundresses, and general maids-of-all-work to the soldiers in camp.

Glossary

abolition Ending slavery.

adobe A building material made out of mud, often mixed with straw and dried in the sun.

assassinate To murder someone by sudden and secret attack.

battery An artillery unit, consisting of a number of guns and their crews.

blockade-runner A sailor or ship that ran through the Union blockade of Southern ports during the Civil War.

breechloader A rifle that is loaded through a chamber in the barrel, not from the end of the barrel.

casualty A soldier lost in battle through death, wounds, sickness, capture, or missing in action.

cavalry Mounted soldiers; the role of cavalry changed considerably during the war.

chaplain A clergyman attached to part of the military.

commandeer To seize private goods for military purposes.

commerce raider A Confederate ship that targeted Union merchant shipping to undermine the North's ability to trade.

commissary A storehouse of goods and provisions for military use.

company A military unit consisting of 50 to 100 men commanded by a captain. There were 10 companies in a regiment. Companies were raised by individual states.

conscription The compulsory enrollment of able-bodied people into the armed forces, usually during a national emergency. Although unpopular, conscription was used by both the Union and the Confederacy.

counterattack To attack the enemy after it has attacked you.

dialect A regional variety of a language, which is usually distinguished by its sounds, grammar, and unique words.

draft A system of compulsory military service.

emancipation Freedom

fugitive Someone who has escaped from captivity, such as a runaway slave

garrison A group of soldiers at a military post

habeas corpus A legal protection against being imprisoned without trial. President Abraham Lincoln was severely criticized for suspending the right to trial in the Union during the war. President Jefferson Davis took a similarly unpopular measure in the Confederacy.

impressment The compulsory seizure of goods by governments for public use.

infantry Foot soldiers.

inflation A rapid and widespread increase in prices.

ironclad A ship protected by iron armor.

kerosene A flammable oil produced by distilling petroleum.

Lost Cause A view of the conflict that emerged in the postwar South that idealized the prewar South as a harmonious and happy society.

lynched Executed by a mob, often by hanging, without legal trial.

merchant ship A vessel that is used to transport trade goods or passengers, as opposed to a warship.

mine Known during the Civil War as "torpedoes," mines are explosive devices, usually concealed, designed to destroy enemy soldiers and transportation.

mortar A type of short-barreled cannon that threw shells in a high arc over enemy fortifications, commonly used in siege warfare.

nativist Someone who supports polities favoring "native" inhabitants over immigrants; "native" Americans did not include indigenous peoples.

neutral Not taking sides.

outhouse An outside bathroom that is not attached to a house.

overseer A supervisor employed to manage workers.

parole Captured prisoners early in the war were exchanged and paroled, which meant they gave their word that they would not fight any more. Union authorities restricted the practice when they realized it was the main means by which the Confederacy replenished its troops.

peddler A merchant who sells his goods by traveling around or going door to door.

prisoner exchange An organized swap of prisoners of war performed by both sides.

prize In wartime, an enemy ship captured at sea.

private The lowest rank in an army.

privateer A pirate given a government license to attack enemy ships and seize their cargo.

profiteering Making unreasonably high profits by selling essential goods at high prices during times of emergency, such as wars.

progressives People who believe that economic development will help introduce beneficial social change.

propaganda Material intended to make readers or observers support a particular cause, often by a biased account of the facts.

Protestant ethics A short-hand term for a view of the world that emphasizes hard work, morality, and sober and modest behavior.

quota A required number of soldiers from each state.

Reconstruction era The period from 1865 to 1877, when the Confederate states were rebuilt and brought back into the Union.

recruit A soldier or other serviceman who has just joined the services.

refugees people who have been displaced from their homes, usually by war or natural disaster.

rout A crushing defeat.

secessionist A person who supported the breaking away of the Southern states from the United States and was thus a supporter of the Confederacy.

segregation The separation of people based on their skin color or another quality.

sentry A soldier standing guard.

siege To surround and cut off supplies to an army or town to force surrender.

skirmish A minor fight.

skirmishers Infantrymen trained to fight in open order rather than the closed ranks of ordinary soldiers. They were often used ahead of the main force to prepare the way for a main attack or as snipers to harass an enemy counterattack.

sutler A camp follower who sold provisions to the soldiers to supplement their army rations. Sutlers usually had a semi-official status and were attached to specific regiments. They were often resented for charging very high prices.

small arms Weapons that are carried and fired by hand

volunteer A civilian who fights when his country goes to war, often because of personal convictions, a sense of adventure, or for a bounty or enlistment fee. The majority of Civil War soldiers were volunteers, rather than regular soldiers.

Further Research

BOOKS

Barney, William L. *The Oxford Encyclopedia of the Civil War*. Oxford University Press, 2011.

Berlin, Ira, et al. (editors). *Free at Last: A Documentary History of Slavery, Freedom, and the Civil War*. New York: The New Press, 1992.

Bynum, Victoria E. *The Long Shadow of the Civil War: Southern Dissent and its Legacies*. University of North Carolina Press, 2010.

Catton, Bruce. *The Civil War*. Boston, MA: Houghton Mifflin, 1987.

Civil War Preservation Trust. *Civil War Sites: The Official Guide to the Civil War Discovery Trail*. Globe Pequot, 2007.

Coles, David J., et al. *Encyclopedia of the American Civil War: Political, Social, and Military History*. W.W. Norton and Company, 2002.

Creighton, Margaret S. *The Colors of Courage: Gettysburg's Forgotten History: Immigrants, Women, and African Americans in the Civil War's Defining Battle*. Basic Books, 2006.

Edwards, Laura F. *Scarlett Doesn't Live Here Anymore: Southern Women in the Civil War Era*. University of Illinois Press, 2004.

Faust, Drew Gilpin. *This Republic of Suffering: Death and the American Civil War*. Vintage, 2009.

Frank, Lisa Tendrich. *Women in the American Civil War* (2 vols). ABC-Clio, 2007.

Goldfield, David. *America Aflame: How the Civil War Created a Nation*. Bloomsbury Press, 2011.

Harper, Judith E. *Women During the Civil War: An Encyclopedia*. Routledge, 2007.

Hendrickson, Robert. *The Road to Appomattox*. New York: John Wiley, 1998.

Holzer, Harold, and Craig Symonds. *The New York Times Complete Civil War 1861–1865*. Black Dog and Leventhal Publishers, 2010.

McPherson, James M. *Battle Cry of Freedom*. New York: Oxford University Press, 1988.

McPherson, James, and James K. Hogue. *Ordeal by Fire: The Civil War and Reconstruction*. McGraw–Hill, 2010.

Mahin, Dean B. *The Blessed Place of Freedom: Europeans in Civil War America*. Potomac Books, Inc., 2003.

Manning, Chandra. *What This Cruel War Was Over: Soldiers, Slavery, and the Civil War*. Vintage, 2008.

Rable, George C. *God's Almost Chosen Peoples: A Religious History of the American Civil War*. University of North Carolina Press, 2010.

Robertson, James I. *Soldiers Blue and Gray*. Columbia, SC: University of South Carolina Press, 1998.

Schecter, Barnet. *The Devil's Own Work: The Civil War Draft Riots and the Fight to Reconstruct America*. Walker & Company, 2007.

Smith, Andrew F. *Starving the South: How the North Won the Civil War*. St. Martin's Press, 2011.

Taylor, Amy Murrell. *The Divided Family in Civil War America*. University of North Carolina Press, 2009.

Trudeau, Noah. *Like Men of War: Black Troops in the Civil War, 1862–1865*. New York: Little, Brown, and Co, 1998.

Varhola, Michael J. *Life in Civil War America*. Family Tree Books, 2011.

Woodworth, Steven E. *American Civil War* (Gale Library of Daily Life). Gale, 2008.

Wright, Mark. *What They Didn't Teach You about the Civil War*. Novato, CA: Presidio Press, 1996.

INTERNET RESOURCES

These general sites have comprehensive links to a large number of Civil War topics:

http://sunsite.utk.edu/civil-war/warweb.html

http://civilwarhome.com/

http://americancivilwar.com/

http://www.civil-war.net/

http://www2.cr.nps.gov/abpp/battles/bystate.htm
This part of the National Parks Service site allows you to search for battles by state

http://pdmusic.org/civilwar.html
Sound files and words to Civil War songs

http://www.civilwarmed.org/
National Museum of Civil War Medicine

http://memory.loc.gov/ammem/aaohtml/exhibit/aopart4.html
Civil War section of the African American Odyssey online exhibition at the Library of Congress

http://valley.vcdh.virginia.edu/
The Valley of the Shadow Project: details of Civil War life in two communities, one Northern and one Southern

http://www.civilwarhome.com/records.htm
Battle reports by commanding generals from the Official Records

http://www.cwc.lsu.edu/
The United States Civil War Center at Lousiana State University

http://www.nps.gov/gett/gettkidz/soldslang.htm
Civil War slang from the site of the Gettysburg National Military Park

http://www.sonofthesouth.net/leefoundation/ebooks.htm
The Robert E. Lee Foundation digital library of books about Lee and about the Civil War generally

Index

Page numbers in *italic* refer to illustrations and captions.

FRIENDS FREE LIBRARY
GERMANTOWN FRIENDS LIBRARY
5418 Germantown Avenue
Philadelphia, PA 19144
215-951-2355

Each borrower is responsible for all items
checked out on his/her library card, for
fines on materials kept overtime, and
replacing any lost or damaged materials.

DEMCO